THE RESTAURANT OWNER'S GUIDE TO

Filling The Dining Room and Profiting Wildly

TIPS, TECHNIQUES, AND STRATEGIES FOR GROWING ANY RESTAURANT EVEN IN THE TOUGHEST ECONOMIES

By John J Racine Jr

978-0-9988599-2-7 Print
978-0-9988599-3-4 Ebook

Library of Congress Control Number: 2018909790

DEDICATION

Dedicated to:

My mom, Sharon, without whom I would not be the man I am today. To my dad, John Sr, who has shown me how to live life without regrets. And to my best friend and business partner, Chad, who is the most generous person and savviest Operator I have ever worked with. He drives me to do more. And to Harriette, a mentor unlike any other. She has pushed me way outside of my comfort zone in business and in life.

TABLE OF CONTENTS

Table of Contents

INTRODUCTION

If someone could wave a magic wand and suddenly change something about your Restaurant, what one thing would you have them change?

Would you have them provide you with an easier way to contact more prospective customers? And would you want those prospective customers as well as your current customers to appreciate and value your establishment more?

Or would it be to have more customers entering your restaurant on a regular basis? Especially on those notorious days, hours and times of year when it is a major challenge to stay busy.

You may be good at the operation you are running, but how would you like to be even better at serving your customers and ensuring their satisfaction? Perhaps you would like to be more effective at advertisements or, is repeat business more important to you?

What if your current customers felt that you were the only person or the only restaurant who understood and could effectively serve their specialized, unique and individual tastes?

Or, how about referrals? Take the best customers you have right now. How would you like to have more contacts just like them? What one thing would you change to make you a better, happier, and more productive restaurant owner?

In the chapters to follow, we'll be discussing not only these areas but other factors that are critical for you to realize real success in your restaurant. Throughout the pages of this manual, we'll explore some of the most effective ideas and field-proven methods and techniques that you can begin to put to use immediately to help you increase your sales, improve your restaurant, overcome some of your most difficult problems and challenges, gain extra income, have more free time, and find a renewed enjoyment from your Restaurant.

Increasing Your Effectiveness

You and I both know that it's no secret that things are changing today, faster than ever before. Technology has become more sophisticated, competition keener, and customers have become more educated and aware.

And with the wide variety of choices your customers have, not only in similar menu offerings from different restaurants, but also in the individual people they deal with, it stands to reason that the more skillful and professional you are at meeting your customer's needs, the bigger advantage you can command, and the more effective and successful you can become.

If you're really going to be effective and successful in the restaurant business today, it is necessary, even vital, that you continually change, improve, adjust and update your menu, service, and communication skills, as well as your methods of marketing and general operation. It has been said, (and you've no doubt heard) that:

**"People don't care how much you know,
until they know how much you care."**

One of the best and most effective ways you can show your prospects and customers you care is by helping them enjoy your menu while also providing outstanding service.

Exposure To New Ideas

And that's what this book is all about. It has been written with the

2

goal of helping your restaurant become the best it can be.

Naturally, this book doesn't claim, nor does it pretend, to have all the answers to all your restaurant's problems. No book, course or seminar could do that.

Rather, the objective of this program is to expose you to some tried, tested, and field-proven ideas, concepts, and techniques that have worked for other restaurant owners much like you.

Once acquainted with new information and ideas, it will then be up to you to decide which ideas can best be tailored to your own restaurant, and how you will begin to use them to better serve your customers and prospects.

The goal of this program is not to try to make you a marketing or restaurant expert, but rather, to provide you with some of the tools the experts and those who are already successful in the industry are currently using.

Together, we'll explore specific marketing, sales, customer service, and business building techniques that others have used to significantly increase their restaurant business and incomes with very little extra effort.

You will most likely find that many of these ideas will be easy to implement, and you'll be able to begin using them right away. Others may take a little longer to gear up for. And still, others may not be right for you or your operation at all. That's okay. It's not possible to provide 100% usable ideas for every person in every situation.

But if you get just one or two good, usable ideas that you can put into your Restaurant's operation that makes a difference, then your time, effort and money will be well invested.

How We Retain Information

Getting a new idea is one thing, but what you do with it once you have it, is just as important as getting it in the first place. Studies on retention show that you remember:

- 10% of what you read,
- 22% of what you hear,
- 37% of what you see,
- 56% of what you see and hear, and up to
- 86% of what you see, hear and do.

So an idea that is heard but not acted on is only half as likely to be retained as an idea that is actually put into practice. With that concept in mind then, it is important to understand that if the information presented in this book is to be of any real value to you, it must not only be read, it must be applied. That is to say, it must be experienced or acted on. And that means it's going to take some effort on your part.

In their book, *The Knowing-Doing Gap,* authors, Jeffrey Pheffer and Robert L. Sutton mention that every year there are 1,700 new business books published, $60 billion spent on training, $43 billion spent on consultants and our universities turn out 80,000 graduates with MBA's. Yet, most businesses continue to operate day in and day out in much the same ways as they've always done.

You see, knowledge without action is no better than no knowledge at all. Just knowing isn't enough. You've got to do something with what you to know.

The ideas presented in this manual work. They're not theory. They're not speculation on what "should" work. And they're not philosophical musings. These ideas, concepts and techniques are currently in use by various business owners (including restaurants) across the country in one form or another. They're being proven in actual field use day in and day out.

They work for others, and they can work for you. But, you're going to have to take the time to study them, understand them and make the necessary modifications to tailor them to your own personal and business style and operation. And then finally, you're going to have to apply them in your restaurant.

Five Steps Of Learning And Retention

Learning - the acquisition of new information or knowledge, and Retention - the ability to capture that information and recall it when wanted or needed, is actually a process that involves five steps:

First, is **Impact.** That is, actually receiving the idea in your mind. Impact can be in the form of a word, a visual observation or a concept. It makes no difference. Your mind isn't capable of making a distinction between a visual or an actual experience. Nor is it capable of determining the difference between a conscious or an unconscious impact an idea may have on you. As far as your mind is concerned, those experiences are all the same and your mind will accept them, regardless.

If information or an experience appears real to your mind, your emotions and nervous system will react as though it were actually real.

To illustrate this point, try this simple experiment:

Seat yourself in a comfortable chair, feet flat on the floor and your hands resting comfortably in your lap.
Close your eyes, take a deep breath, let it out slowly and relax.

Take another one. Let it out slowly. Relax even more.

Visualize a lemon resting on a table in front of you. Visualize it.

See it clearly. Look at its shape – its color – its texture.

Now, mentally reach out with your hand and pick up the lemon. Bring it up to your face. Look at it closely. Squeeze it. Do you notice how firm it feels? Feel the texture of the lemon's dimply and waxy skin. Notice the lemon's yellow color and round shape, with its pointy ends.

Now, hold it up to your nose. Smell it. Do you notice the lemon's citrusy smell?

Place the lemon on the table and mentally pick up a knife that's laying nearby. Cut the lemon in two.

Pick up one half of the lemon and see the juice dripping from it. Bring the lemon up to your nose. Smell it again. Now bite into the lemon.

What's happening to you right now? Is saliva flooding your mouth, both in your mind, as well as physically?

Now consider what just happened. In actuality, there was no lemon. You just pictured one in your mind. While this was just a mental exercise, and the lemon was just imagined, chances are, if you are like most people, the mental image you were playing on the screen of your mind triggered certain responses which manifested themselves physically. So, you can see by this demonstration, that *Impact* is a critical step involved in the process of learning and retention.

The second step is **Repetition.** One university study revealed that an idea that was read or heard only one time was 66% forgotten within 24 hours. But if that same idea was read or heard repeatedly for 8 days, up to 90% of it could be retained at the end of the eight days.

So once you've read this book all the way through, go back and read it again. But this time read with a highlighter, a pencil, and a notepad handy. Mark up the book. Write down the ideas you feel fit your personal business situation. This repetition will help you retain more of the information than if you had read it only once.

The third step in the learning and retention process is **Utilization.** This is the "doing" step. It is here that neuromuscular pathways are actually developed, creating a "mind-muscle memory." And according to the study quoted earlier, once you physically experience an action, it becomes twice as easy to recall as if you had heard it only.

Fourth, is **Internalization.** Actually making the idea a part of you. That may involve some customizing or tailoring of the idea to fit your situation or style, but it is vitally important for you to personalize the idea and make it "yours."

The fifth step is **Reinforcement.** In order to maximize the effectiveness of an idea, you should continually be looking for ways to support and strengthen it. The more you can support the idea, the more you will believe it, the longer you will retain it, and the more effective it will become in helping you serve your customers' needs.

Now, what does all this have to do with your restaurant? Simply, this. In your daily restaurant business and personal activities, as well as throughout your experience with the information presented in this book, you are going to be exposed to a great number of ideas.

Some will be brand new, that is, you've never heard them before. Some will be ideas you have heard in the past, but have forgotten. And others will be ideas you come up with on your own as a result of something that was triggered in your mind as you read. Understanding and applying these five steps in the learning and retention process can help you retain more of what you read and experience.

Action Makes the Difference

It's important to keep an open mind as you read, hear, or otherwise experience ideas that can help you. Try not to judge them or cast them aside too quickly because they don't sound good, they're not part of your personality or makeup, or because you may have heard them before.

Instead, consider these courses of actions:

If you've heard an idea before, say to yourself, "Yes, I've heard that before, but am I using it?" If not, "Why not?"

If you are currently using the idea, ask yourself, "How effective am I at using it? How can I 'plus', or improve on it to make it even more effective for me and my business?"

Next, ask yourself this question: "What will I do as a result of what I've learned?"

Remember, it's not *what* you know – it's what you *do* that counts.

Ideas are powerful. And good ideas are really important for any business. They're what keeps your interest up and your business fresh and alive and growing. And put into action, good ideas can make a huge difference in the way you run your Restaurant, the results you realize, the fun you have, and the profits you make.

This book is full of good, practical, and usable ideas that can help make that big difference for you. But it's up to you to tailor them to your own unique situation, and more importantly, to put them into action.

The Business You're In

If you don't learn another thing from our time together, remember this...

You're NOT in the restaurant business...
You're in the *MARKETING* business.

Read those sentences again... and again... and again. Digest them. Understand them. Internalize them. Make them an integral part of your business philosophy. Because unless and until you do, your business will be no better and no different than any of the other choices your prospects and customers can select to patronize.

Let me explain by using the insurance profession as an example, and as I do, think about how these principles might apply to your restaurant.

It's a well-known fact that very few people (if any at all), want to actually buy an insurance policy. It's true, they may want the benefits, security, and peace of mind that insurance provides them and their families or their business, but they don't necessarily want to spend their money on an insurance policy. But, what do most insurance salespeople sell?

They sell insurance!

No wonder the business is so difficult. It doesn't take a Harvard degree to figure it out. If you sell insurance... and know that people don't want to buy insurance... why would you continue to beat your head against the wall trying to sell it?

Consider the way most people shop for auto insurance. They call up a number of insurance companies and ask for a quote. The agent or his or her representative asks what coverage the caller is currently carrying, and gives a quote based on those figures.

The caller then thanks the agent or staff member, and goes to the next number on their list. More so nowadays, they are probably getting online quotes. Anyways, they keep repeating that scenario

9

until they're convinced that they've found the lowest price... and whichever company comes in lowest gets the business. Use the internet and most of this scenario simply goes away.

But, wait a minute. Isn't there more to buying insurance than just "low price?" Well, sure there is. And you and I both know it. And so do most insurance agents.

Why is it, then, that nearly every agent from nearly every insurance company you call tries to sell on price... knowing that there's probably someone out there with a lower price than they can quote?

Why is it that so few agents try to differentiate themselves from their competition, and change the prospect's base of thinking away from price, and on to other, more important things?

Price is important, don't get me wrong. It's very important. And it carries a lot of weight in a prospect's buying decision.

But it's only one of many factors that a person needs to consider when making their buying decision.

In actuality, there's very little difference in insurance policies issued by any number of insurance companies in the same geographical area.

And likewise, there's usually very little difference in the products or services you sell versus those same types of products or services sold by your competitors.

General overhead costs, utilities, phones, supplies, wages, and product costs are also similar for most companies that sell like products and services.

So, if all those factors... the similarity of products and services, overhead costs and product costs... are pretty much the same, the prices charged by each individual business must, out of necessity, be pretty close, as well. Your Restaurant is no different...

It's true, that one company may, for example, obtain a lower purchase price on their products and as a result, be able to offer a more attractive sales price for a certain period of time, but eventually, things change and the playing field becomes pretty level once again.

There are other factors not to be overlooked such as investment income and tax write-offs or advantages that can play a role in the prices businesses charge for the things they sell.

But overall, all things considered, the prices charged for the goods and services from one company to another similar company are going to be fairly close over the long haul.

The point is,

You will never maintain, long-term... a competitive advantage because of the products you offer, or the prices you charge.

As soon as you develop a new menu item, or offer a new delivery service, it's just a matter of time before your competition latches on to it and offers the exact same thing, or maybe enhances it and offers it for a lower price. And as soon as you lower your prices, your competition can do the same thing.

The marketplace you operate in is so fiercely competitive, so cutthroat, so unforgiving that you absolutely *must* do something to differentiate yourself from your competition.

If you don't, you'll be relegated to just another "me-too" restaurant like all your competitors.

Now, do you want to know the good news?

That's how your competitors operate- in a "ME-TOO!" manner.

Just look around. They're all the same. Their restaurants all look the same. Their menus are all the same. They walk and talk the same. And their advertising all looks like and says the same things as the next guy's if they are even advertising at all. And because they all operate that way and don't know how to change… it gives you a tremendous opportunity!

You see if they keep on doing what they've always done… they'll keep on getting what they've always got.

But if you want to get something different, you've got to be willing to make some changes. And that's what this program is all about. Making changes… changes that will produce real and measurable results in your Restaurant business.

But, what you'll learn here isn't enough. These ideas and strategies alone won't work. You've got to take action on them if you expect anything different than what you're currently getting.

So, make the action commitment now… and let's get started!

"Brain cells create ideas. Stress kills brain cells. Stress is not a good idea."

Richard Saunders, aka Poor Richard

1

ACHIEVING OUTSTANDING RESTAURANT SUCCESS

Personal Traits of Exceptional Performers

Some time back a friend of mine had the awesome opportunity of having dinner with his friend Earl Nightingale, the famous radio personality and producer of self-improvement cassette programs.

Earl made his life's work studying successful people and how they achieved their successes. My friend had long admired Earl for his ideas and philosophy.

And on that occasion, my friend asked him what advice he would give his young son if he had one. What, based on his vast experience and knowledge, would be the one thing that would help his son ensure success both in business as well as in his personal life.

Earl told my friend, "You know, I have often thought about that very question. And after all the years and all the study, I've come to the conclusion that your success in life, or in business for that matter, can be boiled down to one thing. That is, your rewards will always be in direct proportion to the amount of service you render.

"You only have to look around," he said. "The people who serve

13

others prosper. The people who don't serve others don't prosper. And you can tell just how successful a person is by the amount of service they render to others.

"The problem," he continued, "is unsuccessful people either haven't learned that great secret or they don't apply it.

"The successful people are the ones who develop the habits of doing the things that unsuccessful people don't do for one reason or another."

What Failures Don't Like to Do

Earl's comments hit my friend like a big hammer that night, as he realized how true they were. The more you serve your customers, and help them satisfy their needs, the more you will prosper.

And as a restaurant owner, manager, professional person or entrepreneur, serving your customer's needs effectively means that you must do the things that unsuccessful restaurant owners, managers, professionals, and entrepreneurs don't do. The things that those unsuccessful people don't do are the things that most of us don't like to do either.

There is no doubt that it is difficult to work long hours or on weekends when your family is waiting for you at home, and only have a couple of "customers" stop by or be stood up for a reservation someone made with your establishment.

It's discouraging to not have your restaurant filled on a Friday or Saturday night, heck, it's discouraging to have your restaurant not filled during any lunch or dinner period when you should have a packed house on a wait.

Enough of these experiences can be discouraging for any restaurant. And after a while, some people just quit trying. They find it easier to adjust their standards much like we see on TV shows like Kitchen Nightmares or 24 Hours To Hell and Back.

They are no longer in control. Oftentimes, the staff is not even in control. That's when we see cleanliness issues, outdated food, and vistors no restaurant wants to see. Fortunately for them, many of their competitors are in the same situation.

Outstanding success is unusual and is dependent on many different factors. For some restaurants, it just happens. They're in the right place at the right time, they do nothing special, everything just falls into place for them. Others put in long hours and much work, only to find average success.

But a clear understanding of success principles, a well developed and executed plan, and certain personality traits and characteristics can help move you towards your goals more quickly.

Here are some personal qualities to consider:

Eight Personal Qualities For Success

1. Know What You Want

Know yourself and exactly what you want and expect out of your restaurant. So many people enter into the restaurant business and spend years in that environment without having any idea of what they want, or what is possible to get out of their restaurants.

In fact, most restaurant owners are working so hard *in* their restaurants that they don't have time to work *on* them. As a result, they've become slaves to them. They've got things backward. They're working for their business rather than their business working for them.

Take the time to carefully analyze where you've come from, where you are now, and what you want to accomplish in your restaurant. Then begin to set some meaningful goals to help you accomplish your objectives. You see, if you don't know where you want to go, you'll have no idea of what to do in order to get there.

Meaningful goals are an essential requirement for success in the restaurant business. With goals, you have a target to aim for, a purpose for being, and a direction to travel. Without goals, it's easy to wander aimlessly, getting sidetracked by any little thing that comes along.

When you set your goals, think of the word, "SMART." You should have SMART goals. That is, your goals should be:

- Specific,
- Measurable,
- Actionable,
- Realistic, and
- Time-bound

It is important for your goals to be *Specific,* so you will know exactly what you're shooting for. Your goal should be clearly defined and identified so you not only know what you are trying to accomplish, you'll also know when you achieve it.

Just to say you want to sell more steaks, or offer more home deliveries isn't enough. You need to clearly specify your goal. Is it 12 more steaks per month? An extra fifty home deliveries? How much specifically?

Whatever your goal, there should be no doubt about what you wish to accomplish.

Your goals should be **Measurable.** That is, there should be a system or method of determining how you are progressing in your efforts for attainment. By clearly defining your goals as discussed in the previous step, you will be more able to measure them. It's important for you to be able to see your current status, as well as your progression towards your goals.

Next, your goals should be **Actionable.** If your goal cannot happen because of a lack of action… then there may be no hope for you to reach it, it won't take long for you to become discouraged, and you will either lose concentration and the drive necessary to pursue your goal, or you will abandon it altogether.

Your goal should be something you can reach with just a little extra effort.

An insurance agency owner I'm acquainted with had a large fire and casualty agency. In order to promote the sale of life insurance to his onboard customers, the agency owner introduced a contest for his agents. The agent who sold the most life insurance would win a trip to Hawaii.

One of the agents who worked for the agency but who had never sold much life insurance decided he wanted to try and win the trip. The qualifications to earn the trip was tough, and were based entirely on the sale of life insurance.

Very few agents in this agency ever earned these types of trips by working the entire year for them, but this particular agent put his mind to it and qualified in only four months.

Considering the agent's past performance with regards to life insurance production, it's questionable whether the goal should have been attainable for him. However, the agent found a motivation within that changed the odds to his favor, and he was able to accomplish in a four-month period, what most agents weren't able to do in an entire year. He not only took action, but he took MASSIVE action to achieve the goal.

In your restaurant operation, you need to make sure your goals are not only actionable but are also matches the following terms:

Realistic. If your goal isn't realistic, that is, if it's not something within your realm of achievement, it's just a matter of time before you'll become frustrated and give up. And that can have a negative effect on you as you begin to think of yourself as a failure, or not being good at setting goals.

Then, because of your negative image of yourself relative to setting goals, you will likely give up setting goals in the future. It's a self-feeding mechanism.

The key to being good at setting and achieving goals is to be realistic in your expectations. Set actionable and realistic goals that can be reached with a small amount of effort.

That builds a success image and enhances your self-confidence in a positive way. Then, the next time, set a little higher goal. Not much higher, just a little higher. Again, one that you know you can take action on. And that adds on to, and builds your confidence, that much more.

The next step is to make your goals,

Time-bound. That is, you should set a time limit for their attainment.

This helps you keep on target, not be distracted, and encourages you to complete something you've started. Not only will this help you to realize success at a pre-designated time, but you will enhance your self-image by accomplishing your goal.

If, for instance, your goal is to sell a certain number of plates of a particular dish, or a predetermined dollar amount of sales this year, break that number down into months, weeks, and even days, if necessary.

A large goal becomes much more manageable in small pieces. The key is to break your goals into bite-size pieces and place a time deadline on them, for their accomplishment.

2. The Ability To Focus

The second quality is the ability to focus. Many people hesitate to go into business because they think they lack the talents and abilities necessary to succeed. They look at others who are successful and think that they must have unique talents or capabilities. But after getting to know that person, they find them to really be quite average.

The main difference is that the successful person has developed the ability to focus. A person of average intelligence who is focused on a clearly identified and specific goal will consistently outperform the brightest people who are not focused on anything specific.

3. Determine The Price You'll Pay

You must determine the price you'll have to pay to be successful. For everything in life, there is a price. And it must be paid before you can realize the rewards. In many instances, it takes sacrifice.

A few years ago, in an effort to get a little exercise and help relieve stress, one of my friends bought his wife and himself matching bicycles. They had fun for awhile, but then a group of experienced riders flew by him one day on their fast, shiny, obviously high-priced racing bikes.

Always a competitive person, my friend decided that he would try to catch them and ride with them. But, try as he might, it was to no avail. Nothing he did would allow him to catch up to them. That ate on my friend for about a week, and it wasn't long before he found himself back in the bike shop getting the specifications and prices of one of those "fast, shiny, obviously high-priced" bikes.

$2,500 later, he was back on the road just waiting for those riders to catch him so he could ride with them. My friend was completely decked out in cycling shorts and jersey, special shoes, helmet and his new 16-speed racer.

Then, one day it happened. The group of riders came up on my friend from behind, and he was determined to keep up with them. But a quarter of a mile later, try as he might, he was "off the back." The riders were gone, never to be seen again. That really irritated my friend.

So he bought several books, obtained some videotapes, and sought out the help of a neighbor who was a pretty good rider. He worked hard trying to develop his cycling abilities. He rode every morning from 4:30 to 7:30, while his family was still asleep.

My friend encountered motorists who didn't like cyclists. Some even went so far as to run him off the road and have bottles thrown at him.

He's ridden in the rain and cold weather, and he's ridden in the 120 degree heat. My friend worked hard and eventually hired a cycling coach to help him develop his skills.

Then he entered a local race, and to his surprise, he won! This encouraged him so he entered another race. Then another. And another. And he kept winning.

With the new skills and confidence he was developing, he entered the state and national championships, placing very high in both. The riders who used to pass him were now coming to him for help and advice. They wondered how he could consistently beat them when he hadn't been riding for nearly as long as they had.

What they didn't understand was that it wasn't how long my friend had been training, as much as what he had put into his training.

It wasn't what he did during the race that counted as much as it was what he did during the long, lonely, solitary hours of training.

It was the sacrifices he made that made the difference between being a social rider or the national champion he eventually became.

The same concept of sacrifice applies to operating a successful Restaurant.

If you want to reap the great and abundant rewards your business can provide you, you're going to have to do some not-so-glamorous things at some not-so-convenient times.

You're going to have to do what Earl Nightingale said. You'll have to do "...the things that unsuccessful business owners don't want to do."

That may mean, depending on the type of restaurant you have or operate, that you'll have to leave the comfort of your dining room or office to visit with people about their needs in their homes or businesses at inconvenient times.

If you have a family, this may prove to be a hardship on you, but if you are just starting out in business, or want to increase your existing business or achieve some new goals, you may have to make that sacrifice.

If you are not willing to make the necessary sacrifices, then you can't expect to be as successful in business as someone who is willing to make those sacrifices.

4. Self Responsibility

You are totally responsible for the success of your restaurant and your life. There are no excuses. There may be setbacks or economic downturns, or problems that affect your business.

Economies change, government policies change, and prospects don't buy from you, and the weather is too hot or too cold.

While those things definitely have an impact on you, the way you do business and the sales you make, it is important to realize that those things are beyond your control, and it's up to you, and you alone, to accept responsibility for the success of your business.

No matter how bad you might have it, no matter what difficulties or challenges you might encounter, let me assure you that there are many people who have had difficulties and challenges far greater than any you are ever likely to encounter, and somehow, they managed to pull through. And you can do the same.

Here's a little credo that can help you. It contains just ten, two-letter words:

"If it is to be, it is up to me."

That simple one line sentence says it all. It places the responsibility exactly where it should be... *directly on your shoulders.*

5. Be Committed

Make a total commitment to your success. Now that you have made the decision to be in restaurant business, be in that business.

Get into it with both feet. Don't let anything hold you back.

Even more than getting in the business, see that the business gets in you.

Make a commitment that you are going to succeed, no matter what.

Don't try to work two different jobs or projects at one time. You can't do either of them justice, and you'll likely end up frustrated and broke, and never know whether or not you could have been successful.

6. The Extra Mile

The sixth personal quality necessary to achieve outstanding success in business is that you must be willing to go the extra mile.

It's the "Under promise, over deliver" concept, and can be summed up in the following statement:

"If you are always willing to do more than what you get paid for, the day will come when you will be paid for more than what you actually do."

Robert Cialdini, in his book, *Influence: The Psychology of Persuasion*, discusses what he calls the Law of Reciprocity. Basically, it says that when you do something for someone else there's an unstated obligation for them to want to do something for you in return.

So, when you go the extra mile for your customers or clients, you've just set the stage for that law to take effect. But it's only on that "extra mile" that this works. When you give what might be considered "normal" service, or "adequate" service or – even "good" service, you haven't earned the right to expect that law to work for you.

In fact, even performing "knock-out" service often isn't enough to gain you an advantage. We've all come to expect that from any number of businesses.

You've really got to do something special in order to gain an advantage in today's highly competitive marketplace. Then, and only then, can you expect to create that nearly compelling desire in your customer to reciprocate. This simple truth says it all:

"There's no traffic jam on the extra mile."

7. Control Your Time

The seventh quality is that you must master and take control of your time. Time is an expendable commodity. Each one of us has the same 24 hours each day. When those hours are gone, they cannot be replaced. They are gone forever, never to be recaptured.

You must treat your time as precious, and guard it wisely and selfishly. Don't let anyone disrupt you or take you away from the focus you have on your goals.

People who don't have goals are used by people who do. If you let others draw you away from your goals, you are simply saying that their goals are more important than your own.

If you are serious about Restaurant business success – really serious, then this is one of the most important and critical areas to defend.

8. Persistence And Determination

Number eight is to develop persistence and determination. From time to time, you will encounter setbacks or reach plateaus where it seems like nothing is going right.

Your competitors lower their prices, run massive ad campaigns and unheard of promotions, and the next thing you know your customers and clients begin doing to patronize them instead of you.

Business is walking out the back door faster than it's coming in the front door.

Your volume is beginning to drop, and you become concerned. You seem to be spending more time in a defensive posture than you do in servicing your existing customers, and you're losing.

Now is not the time to give up. Now is the time to dig in and begin to play offensively.

To be determined not to lose your good customers who you worked so hard to get, your strategy should be to keep in touch with them and continue providing exceptional service.

Nearly every business is cyclical. Eventually, things will change. While you can't be competitive on price all the time, you can becompetitive in the service you give, and the empathy you have for your customers and their problems.

We'll talk more about how to do that in a later chapter, but for now, just resolve in advance; that no matter what, you'll never give up.

Six Personal Abilities Help Guarantee Results

In addition to those eight personal qualities, there are six additional abilities that can help you achieve even greater success:

1. Effective Communication

First, is the ability to communicate effectively with others. You must be able to interact with other people on their level, so they understand you and the points you are trying to get across to them.

Remember that everyone is different. Each of us has different communication and behavior styles, and you need to be versatile enough to relate to each person according to their individual style. Be careful that you speak a language that they are familiar with and can relate to when they hear it. Don't overuse "buzz words," or industry jargon.

2. Stay On Target

This is the ability for you to quickly make midstream corrections. Each one of us is human, and are subject to the frailties that accompany this mortal life. From time to time, we all make mistakes or errors in judgment.

Making the mistake or the error is not the problem – the first time. It's when we keep making the same mistakes over and over again, without learning from them, or that we fail to quickly recover and make the necessary corrections to avoid total calamity, that we run into problems.

3. Develop Foresight

The ability to spot and analyze trends. To be able to look at the past as well as what is happening today, and predict what might happen in the future, can have a significant impact on your Restaurant business success. Another word for this skill is "foresight."

In a recent interview, the president of a very large meat company told how just a few years ago, their largest selling items were canned hams. But today, with more women working, and less time to spend in the kitchen, they sell very few canned hams.

Today their mainstay is precooked dinners. Without foresight, or the ability to look ahead and predict with reasonable accuracy what may happen in the near future, a company could lose its competitive position and find itself in serious trouble.

As a Restaurant owner, you should give serious thought to keeping abreast of industry changes, new laws, tax laws, buying trends, and other factors that could affect your customers either positively or negatively. Then take whatever steps are necessary to prepare yourself to address those changes, as well as posture yourself in the minds of your customers as the expert they've come to know and depend on.

4. Demonstrate Leadership

The fourth ability or skill to develop for outstanding success is that of leadership. Leadership is the ability to take charge and move others to action.

When you are working with a prospect, client or customer, and have identified and analyzed their needs, it is up to you to prepare and recommend a good, workable plan or proposal that will help satisfy those needs; a plan that's right for their situation and that fits their budget.

It's not always up to the customer to tell you what they want. You are the professional. They have come to you for food AND service. You've got a lot more experience, knowledge and understanding of

27

your products and services and what they can do for them than they do. It is up to you to take charge and assume responsibility for the satisfaction and solving of their problems, needs and wants.

And if you approach it with the right mix of professionalism, knowledge and confidence you'll be amazed at how many people will take your advice and follow your leadership.

5. Persuasive Selling Skills

The ability to sell well. It is surprising how little most people in restaurant business know about professional selling. Not surprising honestly. Many restaurant owners believe they are in the food service business, which is only partially true. Selling is one of the most important skills you as a professional business person can possess.

Many of your prospects and your existing customers know just enough about what your products or services can do for them to be dangerous. They have talked to other people, read a few articles in some magazines, may even have seen a program or two on television, checked things out on the Internet, and they think they know exactly what they need. In some cases, they may be close.

But in other cases, they're far from the mark. You owe it to your customers to be as effective a salesperson and Restaurant owner as you can be. By doing that, you'll end up giving them better solutions and better value, saving them both time and money, and helping them have greater peace of mind knowing they have the quality meals and superior service that are best for them.

They will also feel good about their choice of meal and dining location, knowing that they have just dealt with real professionals who really care about them.

You will be a beneficiary of that effort, too. You will you feel good about yourself and the job you have just done for your customer, and that will cause you to be more effective and professional with your next guest. Not only that but your customer, being satisfied with what you have done for him or her, will be more inclined to tell others of their experience.

Believe me, people respond to the personal experiences of people they respect. And they'll respond to you because a real professional and caring person or business is hard to find these days.

6. Action

The sixth ability to develop is that of action. All the things we've discussed in this chapter will do neither you nor anyone else (your customers, for instance) any good if you don't take action and do something about them.

Remember, action is the key. As we discussed earlier, it's not what you know, it's not what you talk about, it's what you do. True success in business, or in life, is an ongoing process. As my friend, Joel Weldon says,

"The Road to Success is Always

Under Construction."

Some people say that knowledge is power. But it isn't. Knowledge is not power unless it's applied. This chapter has supplied you with some vital knowledge necessary to be successful in business. You now have the knowledge – now it's up to you to put that knowledge into action.

"Laughter is the shortest distance between two people."

Victor Borge

2

HOW DO YOUR CUSTOMERS SEE YOU?

Establishing A Positive Identity In The Minds Of Your Customers

Think of the word, "Professional." What image comes to your mind? Do you visualize a doctor, a dentist, a lawyer, or perhaps the president of a large corporation?

Did the image of the owner or manager of the restaurant you run cross your mind?

What criteria do you use to define a "professional?"

What about other people – your customers, for example?

How do you think they define a "professional?"

The meals you prepare for your customers on a daily basis can have a big impact on them and everyone in their universe including, their family, their staff, employees or customers (if they have businesses), and even their financial futures.

The way you run your business and handle your customers' needs on a daily basis says a lot about you and the position you occupy in their minds.

In truth, your occupation should be viewed as being just as "professional" as that of any other, including doctors, dentists, lawyers, or any other type of business head.

The critical question is, how professionally do you perform within the scope of your occupation? How about your staff?

While this program is not a sales training course, it's important to know that no matter what your role in a restaurant is, you're involved in sales in one form or another.

And if you have staff or employees who are involved in sales, it's important for you to know the following information. Yes, servers and bartenders are at the end of the day, salespeople.

Sales in a Restaurant

I have come across far too many "Order Takers" during my career in restaurants and as an avid restaurant diner. Now, to be fair, there is nothing wrong with an order taker. I mean, they take your order and deliver it to you, hopefully with a smile and occasional drink refills.

But does this go far enough today? Me thinks not. You got into the restaurant business for any number of reasons but at the end of the day, this business boils down to a couple of simple things: revenue and profit.

Let me paint a typical scenario of an order taker:

"Hi, welcome to our establishment. What can I get for you today?"

Did this person do anything wrong? No, not necessarily. The guest was greeted and there was an offer of service.

It certainly could have been better though. How about this:

"Hi, welcome to our establishment. My name is John and I will be taking care of you today. May I offer you an ice cold beer or crisp chardonnay while you look over our menu?"

What do you think? Yes, this is definitely better. This is typically the expectation of most restaurant owners and managers but it happens so infrequently.

Let's dig in a little more to really showcase sales as a server or bartender.
"I'd like a rum and coke".

"Excellent choice, Bacardi or Ron Diplomatico?"

Notice what happened there? Your well rum was not even mentioned. This alone results in a higher check average because of the premium offering rather than a well liquor.

You may be thinking the guest did not want the premium liquor. You may be right but my years of experience in the industry says the guest will tell you if they only want the well rum.

Moving on, how about this:

"Would you like to start with an appetizer today?"

Again, pretty typical of most restaurants but not the best way to get the upsell versus:

"What can I bring you from the appetizer menu?

Notice the pattern here, we never want to ask a question that can have a NO as a response. In this case, the choices are not yes or no but rather, soup, salad, chicken wings, quesadilla, etc.

This is just a sampling of what can be accomplished with the right training, leadership and mindset in your restaurant.

How Do Your Customers See You?

How do your customers see you? I mean, when the people you deal with on a regular basis, your customers and prospects – when they view you as the person they do business with, or as the person they are considering doing business with? Who do they see?

Are you someone they might classify as a "typical restaurant owner" – someone who is out to sell them another pedestrian meal, or who is interested more in the sale?

Or do your customers and prospects view you more as an oasis with relaxation and amazing service – someone they like and can relate to and who is genuinely interested in them, and making sure they have the right experience for their individual and specific needs, at the best possible price? And in the event that what they've purchased does not, or will not meet their expectations, or if you're not satisfied for any reason, will be behind you making things right?

How you answer this basic and important question is critical to your success in the restaurant business. It can mean the difference between enormous success, mediocrity, or even dismal failure.

And, it's a self-feeding mechanism, as well. If you are viewed by your customers as a time waster or a food-hustler, even if it is not stated, you will tend to pick up that message yourself and act accordingly, thus reinforcing your customer's image of you.

On the other hand, if your customers welcome you as a member of their family so to speak – someone with their best interests in mind – someone who can help them get a great meal with outstanding service, they will feel good about you. And consequently, you will also feel good about yourself, and the role you play relative to your customer. You will be, and act more professionally, more confident, and will be better able to help your customer with the solving of his or her needs and problems.

As you improve, you can't help but reinforce and strengthen that positive image in both you, and your customer's minds. This goes a long way in helping your Restaurant grow.

What Your Customers Really Want

As a restaurant owner, it is important for you to understand that only 35% of the reason people patronize your restaurant is the menu you offer.

The other 65% of the reason they patronize, is for what you can do or provide for your customer beyond the food and drinks, and what that does for the customer.

In other words, if you are trying to sell your customers and prospects *meals*, you are wasting your time. They are only 35% interested in *that*.

But they are 65% interested in the benefits of *having you involved, the experience...*

You see, chances are good that your customers and prospects can buy the same food (or at least comparable ones) from any one of several of your competitors.

And with that, your competitor may offer a number of additional advantages, as well.

They may have a lower price, better quality, some added bonuses or extras, a location that's more convenient, or options that fit their budget better.

In today's tough, competitive market, it's difficult to compete on price or product. You may be able to command a certain advantage for a period of time because you have a lower price than your competitors, but you and I both know that it will be short-lived.

The truth is, you will never be able to maintain a competitive position in the marketplace – long-term for any length of time because of the prices you charge.

It'll just be a matter of time before either one of your competitors lowers their prices or duplicates (or even betters) yours, or you raise your prices because you no longer have the necessary margins to justify your prices.

But there's one thing your customers can't get from any of your competitors. And that's you, and the empathy, the expertise and the knowledge, education and commitment to service that you bring literally to the table.

Food and Drinks, or Experience?

So it is important to continually ask yourself (and be honest) the following question...

**"How do your customers... the people
who do business with you... your**

On the next page is an example of an easy method you can use to find out.

Take a sheet of paper and draw a line down the middle.

On the left-hand side at the top, label the column, "Food and Drinks."
Label the right-hand column, "Experience"

Every time you are in contact with a customer or prospect, whether they call you or you have them in your restaurant, evaluate the overall purpose of the call/visit.

Food and Drinks	Experience
||||| ||||| ||||	||||| ||||| ||||| ||||| ||||| ||||| ||||| ||||

Did your customer or prospect look to you for the food or drinks you provide? Or did they seek an experience?
Once you've determined that, place a mark in the appropriate column. Then at the end of the month, evaluate the results of your list.

If you have more marks in the "Food & Drinks" column than in the "Experience" column, you pretty well know what perception your customers have of you.

Let me give you a real example. At the time of the writing of this book, I am located in South Florida, specifically the Fort Lauderdale area. I grew up in Rhode Island and there are certain foods I used to eat back in Rhode Island that are simply not available everywhere.

That was until I found a little place nearby called Busters Doughboys and Clam Cakes. This restaurant was opened and is run by Rick, an owner who also hails from Rhode Island and has a ton of classic New England/Rhode Island fare on the menu.

This place is a goldmine of the cuisine from "back home" like chowda(official pronunciation), fish and chips, doughboys, Maine lobster, New York System Weiners(yes, these are a Rhode Island staple) and a host of others.

The first time I went, I was excited about the food, but when I walked in the door, I was instantly transported back to Rhode Island. Pictures on the wall of some of the classic locations I grew up with like the Rocky Point Chowder House, the Crescent Carousel, Salty Brine the radio DJ who every child used to listen to on the radio to hear if school was canceled because of snow and especially to hear him say, "No school Foster-Gloster" etc.

All of the trappings around the restaurant began a feeling of nostalgia and like I was back in RI. Then, the service just took me over the top. I go frequently and Savannah is usually my server. She provides service like I remembered growing up and which got me interested in the industry.

This my friend, is the experience that can be created in a restaurant. Now, what experience are YOU providing in yours?

Improvement is not always difficult. Oftentimes, a person may not know where they are weak or where they need to improve. But if you can isolate those areas that need improvement, you can then begin to take the necessary steps to effect positive change.

"Do what you do so well that they will want to see it again and bring their friends."

Walt Disney

3

DISNEY'S LAW CAN WORK FOR YOU!

Strategies for Determining and Increasing Your Value to Your Customers

Read the quote at the top of the page from Walt Disney. Walt is by far my biggest idol. I have been a fan since I got to travel to Orlando Florida at the ripe old age of 10 and got to visit Walt Disney World for the first time.

It was hard not to be awed at everything I saw on that first visit, especially from the eyes of a 10-year-old. In fact, I was so taken by the trip, I decided then and there I was going to work there when I was an adult.

I picked my college and major based on getting hired at Disney. I went to school at Johnson & Wales University in Providence and I picked Culinary Arts and Hospitality Management as my majors. I did my research on how Disney did their recruiting and made sure I was somebody they wanted to hire.

I am happy to report Disney did feel I was worthy of review and offered me a position as a Restaurant Manager, straight out of college.

Once I stepped foot into the role, I received a world class education in how to take care of customers, or as they are called at Walt Disney World, guests. I have carried that experience through with me to every job I had and even now as a business owner.

Back to the quote, "Do what you do so well they will want to see it again and bring their friends". It can be the same in your restaurant business too. You see, the key is to "*do what you do*," not what someone else does, but what *you* do. You don't have to copy. You simply do your job the way only you can. That's what makes you special, sets you apart from others, and attracts people to you.

Then you do what you do, "*so well*," that is, provide the type of service your customers require, want, or need in an exceptional manner. It leaves no room for mediocrity, it's "so well." That implies exceptional performance.

And if you will do that so, "*the people who see you do it*," (your customers), "*will want to see you do it again*," (that's repeat business), "*and will bring others to see you do it*," (that's referral business), you too, can meet with an unparalleled success.

Because so few people perform in business that way, it sets you completely apart from all the competition. Customers can't get the kind of service you offer from anyone or anywhere else. It's simply not available anywhere, at any price.

So, by default, you become unique, different, and difficult to replace. And it will be reflected in your business and your income. It has to. There's no choice. It is a basic, eternal law of nature. You simply reap the results of what you've sown.

You Reap What You Sow

The question you must answer in your mind is, "What are you going to sow, so you will reap the kinds of rewards you wish to have?"

In the restaurant business, this is a most critical question and one you would do well to take the time to answer. Fact is, most business people simply don't understand how important the answer to this one question really is.

You see, many people go into business because it is something they have always wanted to do, or because they want a certain amount of freedom, or perhaps they want to be their own boss.

Now, those are not necessarily bad reasons, but they are selfish reasons for the most part, and while they may sound good on the surface, in actuality, some of them may not be very practical.

If you go into business for selfish reasons, and fail to give the customer his or her rightful due, your chances of success are likely to meet with hard times.

Business, like farming, requires that you do certain things in a particular order if you are to realize an abundant harvest. Now the answer to the question,

"What are you going to sow, so you will reap the kinds of rewards you want?"

…is simple. You only have to look at the question backwards. First, what kinds of rewards do you want? Second, what do you have to do to get those rewards? And third, who is it that can give you those rewards?

If you will always remember that although you may own or work for, or represent, a certain company or organization, they are not who pays you.

The Customer Signs Your Paycheck

It really is the customer that signs your paycheck. And although you must see that your company's interests are always considered, you must not lose sight that the customer is the boss.

They are the whole reason your job exists in the first place. They want food and or drinks. They want it served in a friendly environment. They also want it presented in an appealing way which has been prepared to their liking. They trust you to help them see that their needs are met or satisfied in an efficient and cost-effective manner, and they pay you well to do your job. It is the wants, needs and desires of your customers that should determine all of your business activity. So the next logical step then, is to learn and understand just what your customer's wants, needs and desires are. And you find that out simply by interviewing and asking them. It is very important to listen carefully to what they say because sometimes there may be other, hidden or unstated wants or needs that may not be readily evident. And only by fully understanding their needs, can you be of meaningful service to them.

4

WHY PEOPLE BUY

Identifying The Basic Motives That Make Your Customers Want To Buy

According to Bon Appetit, what keeps people coming back to the restaurants they love? In some cases, it's exceptionally delicious food. In others, the allure isn't about the food at all. Perhaps it's a favorite server, or the feeling of being recognized by everyone on staff when you walk through the door. Maybe it's just an inexplicable feeling of homeyness they haven't been able to find in any other restaurant. These aren't things you can eat, but they're every bit as critical to a restaurant's success (or failure) as its food.

This should cause you to really evaluate what it means to be in the restaurant industry. What this essentially translate to is people are not frequenting your restaurant for the food. I have been beating that drum for years and throughout the pages of this book.

Let me show you an example from outside of the foodservice industry. The example that has traditionally been used to illustrate this point is that one year, a quarter of a million quarter-inch drills were sold, and not one person that bought a drill wanted a quarter-inch drill. Instead, they bought the drills because they wanted the benefits the drill could provide... a hole.

People buy your products and services for the same reason - the benefits those products or services provide.

Again, this is no different in the restaurant industry. People are buying an experience, a memory, a flavor, or any number of items not directly related to thirst or hunger. Yes, thirst and hunger play a role but it is far from the primary role for a majority of restaurant patrons.

People Buy For The Benefits

If you ask me why I go to Busters, the restaurant I mentioned in a previous chapter, it is not primarily for food or drink. It is the benefit of nostalgia. Every single dish on the menu reminds me of my youth and the places I used to go back home.

Can another seafood place offer me that nostalgia? None of the bug chain restaurants can. I have been to dozens and dozens of places, but none offer me THAT feeling, or benefit.

What benefit do you offer in your restaurant? Is it a taste of home, a server that takes care of you like family, or is it something else?

Is the benefit the biggest value available in town much like a grand buffet in Las Vegas? Or is it the benefit of serving one of the most expensive menu items anywhere much like a high-end Japanese Wagyu steak or rare pour of Scotch?

What the Heck is a USP?

There is an acronym that those if us in marketing and helping businesses to grow and prosper use on a pretty regular basis and that is USP. It stands for Unique Selling Point or Proposition.

Wikipedia.org defines a USP as:

"A unique selling proposition (USP) refers to the unique benefit exhibited by a company, service, product or brand that enables it to stand out from competitors. The unique selling proposition must be a feature that highlights product benefits that are meaningful to consumers."

How can you have a USP in a restaurant much like other restaurant in your community? The real question is, how can you not?

Let me give you an example of a USP from a pretty mundane restaurant. This restaurant serves meatloaf, fried chicken, pot roast with all the fixin's and classic milkshakes. Sounds pretty normal and pedestrian, right?

So what is their USP? Classic American comfort food, '50s kitsch and a good old-fashioned family gathering take you back to a bygone era. This is the USP for the 50's Prime Time Diner at Walt Disney World. They are serving up traditional 1950's fare but have added the décor and environment to create a truly unique experience.

You can easily create your own with ANY kind of restaurant. It only takes some ingenuity and not a large bank balance.

Treat your customers like your closest family and you have created a USP. Serve a regionalized menu not typically found in your area, you have created another USP. Offer the most value driven menu, bang another USP. Make your dining room an ode to the hunting lodges of the great northern states, you have yet another USP. See? It's actually pretty easy.

Motives For Buying

Behavioral psychologists tell us there are seven basic motives that move a person to action – that cause them to buy. An understanding of these motives and how they apply to your customers and prospects at the time a buying decision is being made can give you a tremendous advantage. Though these are more common in a traditional brick and mortar retail or online business, there are many parallels for the restaurant owner.

Let's drill down...

1. Desire For Gain Or Profit

Nobody likes to lose. People want something in return for their efforts and hard work. And the easier they can get it, the better. The success of the lottery games in various states bears testimony of people trying to find an easy way to get gain and profit.

The products you sell can help your customers realize their dreams for gain or profit, too. Your customers can and will invest in various types of products (meal) or services you sell – not to own them, per se, but in an effort to increase their profitability and the amount and value of their assets.

This definitely applies more the Uber Eats and Grub hubs of the world as they are charging a premium from your menu pricing to deliver to the customer.

I remember very early in my restaurant career, I worked at a restaurant in Jacksonville, Florida which partnered with a company called Take Out Taxi. They were certainly a precursor to today's food delivery services.

Take Out Taxi received a discount on our posted menu pricing and charged the customer the listed menu price. They then charged a delivery fee. So if the menu discount was 20%(I do not recall the exact amount years later), they had a built in revenue stream. I suspect strongly the delivery fee covered the mileage owed to the driver. I may be wrong here, I was not involved in their business model though I could have helped them stay viable in the Jacksonville market.

Oh well.

2. Fear Of Loss, Or Need For Security

People will go to great lengths to prevent losing something. In an effort to protect their property, some people install burglar or fire alarms, smoke detectors, or night lights that automatically come on when movement is detected.

Some people carry spray cans of mace, or tear gas, while others have resorted to carrying guns or other weapons to protect their person.

Psychologists say that the fear of loss or the need for security is perhaps, the greatest of all the motives.

This relates to your restaurant business in the sense that people can buy your products (meals) to save themselves from hunger. They can also buy takeout on their way to work (if they love your food and if it satisfies them) so they do not have to buy and eat things they don't like.

You can exploit this when marketing your restaurant and your menu to them. Convenience is a huge differentiator today. The pace of life has picked up to near space shuttle launch speed which has fueled the growth of companies like Uber Eats and Grub Hub amongst others.

Security also plays a factor with a family. Parents want to make sure the children are well fed and taken care of. When the kids are safe and happy, very often mom and dad are too. This is a bit of an emotional tug but there are many restaurants that use this strategy.

3. Pride Of Ownership, Or Status

People want to be noticed and recognized. Little boys ride bicycles with no hands, and little girls dress up and act out dance routines and shout to their parents, "Watch me! Watch me!"

Adults do the same things but in different ways. While they may not verbally shout out, they still say "Watch me! Watch me!" just as loudly.

They do it by the kinds of cars they drive, the clothes and jewelry they wear, the houses they live in, and the material things they possess.

While people may buy because of the benefits, they like others to see the actual product. In some cases, it's just another way to say, "Watch me! Watch me!"

Your restaurant business should be well branded so that people will be proud to show any souvenirs that prove they have frequented your restaurant. This can often be done through social media by a Check In.

There is a restaurant I have tried to get a reservation to for years. It has a very small dining room, only 60 seats, and is damn near impossible to get a reservation for. In fact, this place is so exclusive, the American Express Platinum Card has 1 table reserved every night for a Platinum card holder. I have never been able to get a reservation on my own or through the Platinum Concierge. That restaurant? The French Laundry in Yountville, California. The heart of Napa Valley.

So when I get that reservation, it would be a pride of ownership situation, no doubt. But, it would be a status thing as well. I was able to get a reservation into one of the most challenging restaurants to get into. Not quite the challenge of Rao's in New York, but still pretty daunting.

4. An Interest In Doing Something Easier Or More Efficiently

We all want methods of doing things easier. One only has to look around his or her home to notice the abundance of time and/or money-saving conveniences we all enjoy. What about your products or services?

Do they somehow make a person's job or a business' way of doing things easier or more efficient?

And if they do, what are the direct and indirect benefits to your prospect or customer?

Is this something you can capitalize on?

You could do home delivery service. You could deliver anywhere within a certain area. You could help reduce the stress of customers having to come all the way to get food.

This theme continues to appear for the purposes of this book and most restaurants. Eating is a necessary evil for some people and cooking is a burdensome chore many people simply won't do. This presents an amazing opportunity for the smart restaurant owner to market and capitalize on a trend that will not slow down or stop anytime in the near future.

5. The Desire For Excitement Or Pleasure

A popular bumper sticker states,

"He who dies with the most toys wins."

That message is a clear indication that people want excitement and pleasure. And it seems to suggest that pleasure comes in the "having," rather than in the "getting." It's whoever has the most at the end that wins.

But in reality, "excitement" and "pleasure," for most people comes in the acquiring of things.

Think back about the times you have worked hard to get something, and how excited you were in the process.

But then, once you had whatever it was that you were working for, how the excitement was dulled.

Sometimes it's not the end result that counts as much as the process of acquiring.

A more practical interpretation of the bumper sticker might read,

"He who lives with the most toys wins!"

Of course, these applications have to do with "things." Some people really enjoy acquiring "things," and even keep score by how much they accumulate.

Other people gain great pleasure or excitement knowing that their family's future educational and livings needs, as well as retirement will be taken care of.

Business owners like to know that their businesses are operating at peak efficiency and profitability, and are meeting the needs of their customers, and as a result, will be around for a long time providing jobs and security for their employees and their families, as well as providing retirement funds for the owner when the business is sold.

Let's take this away from "things" and focus on the pleasure. Restaurants don't typically have "things" unless you are a tourist restaurant with a gift shop much like Planet Hollywood or Hard Rock Café.

Pleasure takes many forms in restaurants. It could be the feeling of having the entire family together on a Friday night at their favorite Mexican restaurant, it could be watching their favorite NFL team on Sunday afternoon at the big sports bar while travelling for work or it could even be that romantic Sunday brunch with a spouse after a previous evening of "Date Night". Restaurants play a very key part in the experience.

6. Self Improvement Or An Increase In Effectiveness

Your investment of both money and time in this book is a good example of your desire for self-improvement and increased effectiveness. People want and need to improve and to be able to do things more efficiently.

Sometimes that involves taking risks with time or money. Not all risks have to be "risky." Calculated risks based on well-thought-out plans and outcomes are the safest way to go and can contribute greatly to the successful improvement in effectiveness and efficiency. I am involved with multiple local marketing and niche focused groups. Many of these groups meet in local restaurants with small groups of people. One of my business mentors started his multi-million dollar speaking business by offering people a free dinner at the local chain breakfast focused restaurant. He paid for all of the dinners and sold an opportunity to get into the real estate investing business. Dave now runs one of the world premier speaker

education companies and it all started at that chain restaurant.

All of the attendees of Dave's dinners were looking for self-improvement. They wanted to make more money. Another friend of mine, Hilda, is an M.D. who left traditional medicine and found a passion for Holistic Medicine. She too uses small local restaurants to offer discovery sessions for prospective patients. These people want to reduce pain, drop weight or just simply live a healthier life. Again, self-improvement.

Is your restaurant courting this type of business?

7. The Desire For Importance Or The Need To Feel Appreciated

According to noted psychiatrist Dr. Abraham Maslow, this is one of the basic needs of all humans; acceptance and appreciation. Children want to be accepted by their parents and peers, and parents want their children to remember them when they grow up and leave home.

In his book, *The Human Side of Enterprise,* Douglas McGregor explains that workers are motivated more by "significant works," and a feeling of being needed and appreciated, than by money.

People want to make a difference and be appreciated for it. Fathers and mothers not only have an obligation to see that their family's futures are provided for, but they want their family to understand and appreciate their efforts.

Restaurant owners have an obligation to the people who buy from them, the employees who work for them, their employees' families, the suppliers and the vendors who sell to them. Too often, each of those groups of people lives with an attitude of expectancy and entitlement. That is, they expect that the business owner will take care of them. How much better it would be if more appreciation would be shown to those who make our lives better.

If the products or services you provide the marketplace can help make this possible, you may have an open ticket to success because of the great unsatisfied need that exists.

If you understand these basic motives and how they apply to your business of selling your products and services and then sell to the needs (both stated and unstated) of your customers and prospects, you will prosper.

And if you are not prospering, it simply means you have not uncovered your prospect's and customer's motives for buying. You are not addressing their specific needs. In most cases, you can't wait for your customers to tell you what they want. You have to be able to recognize their needs.

Remember, you are ultimately responsible for the success or failure of your business. If you are doing it right or wrong, either way, the marketplace will let you know.

The Loyalty Of The Customer

Customers make an interesting study. It seems that they always want the very most for the very least they'll have to pay. They are ruthless, selfish, demanding and disloyal.

You know the story. You've done business with someone for several years and they've been good customers. You've given them the best service possible and you think they are your customers for life. But then some little thing possibly out of your control goes wrong, or they see an ad with a slightly lower price, and the next thing you know, they are gone, oftentimes without a single word to you.

At first, you don't notice it. But one day you realize that it's been a while since you've seen or heard from that customer. When you find out what happened, you feel bad, because if they would have just called you, you might have been able to make a couple of changes and save the business. But it's too late, they're gone.

This scenario is repeated time and again with businesses owners from every company, who sell every type of product or service. It is going to happen. To pretend that it doesn't, or won't happen, is simply deceiving yourself.

Many a restaurant owner dreads the complaints. When I got started in the business, I did too. I simply did not understand the value of the complaint. I was not aware to the fact the complaint oftentimes allowed me to keep that customer for the long term by fixing what caused them to be upset.

Now not every complaint is a legitimate one, but that is part and parcel of being a business owner, especially a restaurant owner. But there are enough of the first type you can use to really impact the customer resulting in a higher lifetime value. More on this later.

It's incredible how many business owners just write off the loss of a good customer. But that's not the thing you should do. Instead, now is the time to become even more proactive and go after that "lost" customer.

One of the best ways to minimize or cut down on the frequency of losing your good customers is to resell them on the reasons they bought from you in the first place. Regularly scheduled conversations with your customers can go a long way in helping insulate your business from the competition. This can be accomplished through regular email communication, an SMS campaign, a print newsletter or simply a phone call. This does require you to have a way to capture this information, but we will dig into that a little later on in this book.

Remember, that your competition has similar products, services, and prices. Also remember that your customer's reasons for buying are only 35 percent based on those products, services, and prices. The other 65 percent is for what you can do for them.

Spend the time with them. Review their needs, wants and concerns. Remind them why they bought from you in the first place. Reinforce their motives and their decisions for visiting, and you will reduce your customer defection rate and develop not only loyal customers but friends, as well.

"In every difficult situation is potential value. Believe this, then begin looking for it."

Norman
Vincent Peale

5

THE MAIN PURPOSE
OF YOUR BUSINESS

Getting And Keeping Customers
Profitability Is Priority Number One

When you have an effective system that will allow you to *profitably* get and keep *quality* customers that will return to do business with you over and over again, and then actively and enthusiastically refer you to others, your business will produce more profits than you can possibly imagine. And then everything else falls into place.

On the other hand, if you don't have enough customers buying from you or using your services regularly, then you'll not likely stay in business for very long and will never have the chance to make a profit.

Now, let's take a minute and look closely at the individual components of this important business skill...

Knowing How To Profitably
Attract Quality Customers

Customers are the lifeblood of any business. Without customers buying, you wouldn't have a business to begin with. But customers alone, aren't enough.

You want *quality* customers... customers who are pleasant to deal with. Customers who return to repurchase from you again and again. Customers who you can sell to and realize a reasonable profit from.

And you want to be able to *profitably* attract them. In other words, the return you realize from your investment in advertising or marketing dollars to acquire new customers should be positive. You want a positive R.O.I. or return on your investment.

Next, you want to...

Ethically Exploit Their
Maximum Financial Potential

Each of your customers has certain needs and wants. And the more of those needs and wants you can handle for them, the more benefits you can provide them, and the more profits you'll realize.

It should be your goal to sell as many products and services to your customers as they need.

You shouldn't take advantage of them or your relationship with them, but you should make every effort to sell them everything that you can *ethically* justify selling them.

It really comes down to this, and I'll speak very frankly. If you really do provide the best products and services in the marketplace (if you don't, you'd better rethink your ethics and why you're in business), and if you really are the business who can serve your customers' needs better than anyone else (and if you're not, you either need to become that business or get out of the business), then you have a moral and an ethical responsibility to make sure that every one of your customers at least has the opportunity to take advantage of them.

And you should do everything in your power that's *reasonable* and *ethical* to give them that opportunity.

Next, you want to…

Convert Your Customers To Advocates Who Actively And Enthusiastically Refer You To Others

By definition, an "advocate" is someone who is a backer, a supporter, a promoter, a believer, an activist, a campaigner, a sponsor.

The last thing you need is a database full of one-product, or one-service customers who buy the minimum amount from you, complain about your prices every time they make a purchase, and give the rest of their business to the company or business who has the lowest prices or a "better deal."

There's no way you can make a profit on these types of customers. Besides, they make your life miserable and drive you crazy in the process.

You need customers who not only give you all (or the majority) of their business, but re-buy from you repeatedly, year after year. You want customers that are so happy and so pleased with what you do for them that they actively and enthusiastically campaign for you. That the story they tell about you is so compelling that the people they tell are nearly forced to call you and ask for your help. Those are the people who make your job fun, enjoyable and profitable.

And finally, you want to...

Keep Your Customers For Life

Reliable studies demonstrate that the more needs a business handles for a customer, the longer they can expect that customer to do business with them.

In the insurance business, for instance, an agent increases his chances of keeping an insured for three years or more by the following percentages:

- 45% if the agent insures only the auto policies
- 50% if both the auto and homeowners policies are insured
- 60% with auto, homeowners and life policies, and
- **97% with auto, homeowners, life and health policies!**

While these figures are illustrative of the insurance business, the same principle is true of most other businesses. Banks, for instance, have studies that show the difference in customer retention with a customer that only has a checking account, versus another customer with multiple checking accounts, a savings account, an IRA, Safety Deposit box, their car financed through the bank, and a number of other services.

This can also work for your restaurant business.

The idea is that by serving all the needs your prospects or

customers have with the products and services you provide or have access to, you lock yourself in and the competition out.

And obviously, the longer you retain your customers, the more income you will earn from them, the more chances you will have to sell them additional products and services, and the more referrals you can get from them. It all adds up to increased profits for you.

Retention of your customers… the ones you've spent so much time, effort and money attracting and convincing to do business with you is critically important.

More than one study suggests that it costs six times more to get a prospect to buy from you than it does to get an existing customer to purchase from you again and that it's sixteen times easier to sell an existing customer than it is a new prospect.

When you add it all up, for every 5% increase in customer retention, you'll generate a 30% to 45% increase in profitability over an 18 month period.

Depending on the nature of the products and services you sell, if your repurchase rate isn't in the high 90 percentile range, you have some work to do.

A lost customer is more than just a lost customer and the attached profits. It's much more. In future chapters, we'll be discussing how to determine what the actual cost of a lost customer is, and what to do to prevent them from leaving.

But for now, just keep this important point in mind… if you're going to be successful in business, no matter what type of products or services you sell, you've got to have an intense focus on your customer. You've got to find out what they want and do everything you can to help them get it.

And if you want to make a fortune rather than just a living, you can't do it for only a few. You must do it for large numbers of people.

The success of your business will depend on how well you serve your customers... the people who buy from you!

"Our deeds determine us as much as we determine our deeds."

George Eliot

6

THE FOUR PRIMARY WAYS TO GROW YOUR RESTAURANT BUSINESS

Maximizing The Return On Your Efforts In The Four Key And Critical Areas

The number one thing… and one of the most important things for any business owner, manager, entrepreneur or professional to realize, is that there are four ways… four *principal* ways to grow a business – any business.

There are many things you can do to grow your restaurant, but for purposes of our discussion here, we'll be focusing on four primary things.

The truth is that other than some administrative functions, some of which are not under your direct influence or control, nearly everything you do to build or grow your business can be classified under one of four different and distinct areas or categories, and if you learn this one simple concept and how to apply it, believe me, your competition won't stand a chance.

And the reason?

Because your competition not only doesn't understand this concept, most of them have never even heard of it.

Now, here's the first one of the four ways to grow your Restaurants. Simply...

Get More Customers

That's it. Build your customer base. Get more prospects to buy from you and become your customers.

You know how it works. When more people buy from you, you take in more gross dollars, and as a result (depending on your margins and overhead), you make more bottom line profits.

As a spin-off benefit, the more people you add to your customer base the larger it becomes, and the larger it becomes the more people you have coming back to you for additional purchases and the referrals they're capable of giving you.

It's in this one single area where most Restaurant owners (including your competition, and probably, you, too, if you're honest), spend most of their time, effort and money.

If you've been in business for any length of time, you probably realize that getting new customers is not always the easiest, the most time-efficient, or most profitable thing you can do.

Most businesses only have one or two main methods of attracting new prospects to their businesses.

For example, you probably know that a large number of businesses are heavy in the use of telephone soliciting.

In fact, you, yourself, have probably gotten more than your fair share of calls, when you were just sitting down for dinner.

Chiropractors, car dealers, truck driving schools, and lawyers take a different approach. Many of them advertise heavily on television, especially during the afternoon hours to attract new customers. They've found that a large part of their intended audience... the people who are most inclined to use their services, watch television during those hours, and it's a cost-effective way to reach them.

Each business, industry, or profession has their own methods and timing to contact those who are most likely to be interested in their products and services. What works for some businesses, may or may not work for other businesses in the same or different industries or professions.

Think about your business and your restaurant for a minute. Chances are, that you, like nearly every other restaurant owner also utilizes one, or perhaps two main methods of attracting new prospects. Maybe Groupon, maybe Facebook, maybe Waze ads or even Google ads.

Most likely, the method you use is the same method that nearly every other restaurant uses. It's called the *"That's how things are done in our industry or profession,"* method.

Typically, when a person first chooses to go into business they look around and see what everyone else is doing.

Then they layout their office, shop or place of business just like every other similar type of business they've seen.

They look at what everyone else is doing to market or promote their businesses, products, and services, and adopt those same marketing plans and methods to market or promote their business.

This activity isn't isolated to just a few businesses – nearly every business in nearly every industry or profession is guilty.

But, wait a minute. Who set up that system in the first place? And who says it's right, or that it's the best system for you to use? The fact is, that there are an unlimited number of methods of attracting new customers to your business, and your imagination is the only limiting factor.

My experience in this industry has shown most restaurants are utilizing each and every one of these strategies the wrong way. Facebook can be a strong generator of new business but not 1 in 100 restaurant owners or managers is utilizing the best and most cost effective way to attract new patrons into their dining rooms.

The same can be said about Google ads. Google is the biggest search engine on earth and has the most robust and diverse advertising platform anywhere. Yet again, there are incredibly few savvy restaurant owners who are utilizing it in the proper way to grow.

Some of the best, most productive and cost-effective methods you can use, can be adapted from what others are doing in totally unrelated businesses.

Now, this brings up a couple of questions. First, how observant are you? What are other restaurant owners doing? And, how effective are they?

Next, look around at what other businesses… unrelated businesses in other, unrelated fields, industries or professions are doing. Have you seen what's working for them? Is there one business that just stands out, by doing something different or unusual? Or, do they all pretty much use the same marketing methods?

Next question: How creative are you? Can you look at what some of the other businesses are doing, and adapt (with a few minor changes), their methods to your business?

In other words, if you were brand new, just starting in business, and had no idea of what anyone before you had done to attract new customers, what would you do? How would you go about getting new customers? Would you use the same methods you use now, or would you do something completely different?

A dentist I consult with specializes in working with children and their teeth. He loves children. And he recognizes that as they get older, they may need braces, they'll probably get married, and have a spouse and children that will all need dental care.

So, he set up his reception room with a special, "kid-height" counter, so when the children come in, they can talk directly to the receptionist, transact their business just as an adult would, and schedule their next appointment. He's even decorated his reception area with artwork and pictures that some of his young patients have created.

How do you think those young people feel? Well, you probably guessed it. They absolutely love it there. And they tell their friends about it, too. And their parents? They're *thrilled.*

Imagine, having your kids *want* to go to the dentist! And then be treated, not like a second-class citizen, but as an equal, transacting business (with the parent's help, of course), and having a hand in scheduling their future appointments.

What a learning and growing experience for them. And who do you think the parents use for their own dentist? That's right.

The spin-off business of catering to, and working with children, is their parents.

As the kids grow up and have families of their own, which dentist do you think they'll use... that they'll insist their spouse switches to, and that they'll bring their own children to?

The relationship this dentist is building with those young people (friendship, trust, and care), will provide him all the financial security he'll ever need, and allow him to do whatever he wants, and go wherever he pleases for the rest of his life.

So, what about you and your business? What are you doing? Specifically, what marketing methods are you using, *right now* to attract new customers, and to build lasting relationships with them so they'll do business with you for a lifetime?

And second, how many *different* marketing methods do you presently, and concurrently, have working for you? There's a real danger in having just one or two main methods of attracting new customers.

One of my consulting clients depended almost entirely on a telemarketing team to acquire leads for their salespeople to follow up with. When a well-funded competitor opened for business not far away, they hired nearly all that business' telemarketing staff, and nearly shut the business down. The business was nearly a total disaster.

When they called me in as a consultant, I could see that we had to do something quick, just to save the business. So, we got to work and hired and trained a whole new telemarketing crew, and got the business up and running again.

But then we looked at other marketing options and put together an effective direct-mail program, used Facebook advertising, started a proactive referral-generating system, and worked out some joint ventures and host-beneficiary relationships with other, complementary, but non-competing businesses.

Now, if something happens to any one of their marketing methods, they have other strategies or other "pillars" in place that can keep the business from collapsing, and keep it running smoothly.

What about your restaurant? How can you apply this?

Well, why not start by going back and revisiting the questions I asked earlier. Then see if there are some areas that you need to improve on.

Make sure you're not dependent on only one or two main methods of attracting new customers.

New customers are important to your business, there's no question. But, they're not just important, they're absolutely vital... not only to the growth of your business but to the very survival of the business.

It's critical that you have multiple systems in place to ensure that your restaurant continues running, *and growing*, uninterrupted if anything unexpected happens.

Because of the limited amount of space in these pages, we can't talk about all the methods of getting new customers, but in the training materials and workshops we conduct, we go into great detail on effective ways to attract prospects by the bushel and convert them into loyal, long-term customers.

As important as getting more new customers is, there are still three more methods you can use to grow your business. And each of these methods is more profitable, more effective, and give you greater potential for leverage than the first method.

Let's talk about number two...

Get Your Customers To Make
Larger Average Purchases

In other words, increase the average check amount. Or more simply, get them to spend more money when they buy something from you.

This just happens to be the quickest and easiest way there is to increase your profits. One of the things that continually amazes me is the number of businesses that have *extensive* and *expensive* plans in place to acquire more customers.

Yet, very few have paid much attention to this highly profitable, and highly leverageable step of increasing the size of the order... getting more money from each of your customers every time they buy from you.

If you think for a minute about how easy this is and how profitable it can be, you'll see why it's such a powerful concept. And, you'll also see why nearly every fast-food restaurant has embraced, has mastered, and requires that every person who takes orders, understands, and is proficient in the use of the "up-sell" and "cross-selling" principles.

Think back about your own fast-food restaurant experience. You drive up to the speaker and place your order... a sandwich and a drink. And then what happens? A voice comes back over the speaker and asks if you'd like an apple pie, or fries with your order.

That's an example of cross-selling. Selling an additional product in addition to, or beyond the initial purchase.

Or, they might suggest that you "super-size" or "giant-size" your order. That's an example of an up-sell... increasing the size of the initial order.

In any case, if you take them up on their suggestion, what they've done is just increase their profits *substantially*, since they made an additional sale, but had no acquisition or marketing costs.

You see, they realize that a certain percentage of their customers will say, "yes." And the only reason they say, "yes," is because a suggestion was made to them. So they play the numbers game.

And the result? Well, by being aware of what their customers might want, but not ask for on their own, and then by asking questions or making suggestions, they bring in a substantial number of dollars. And other than the actual cost of the product, those dollars are pure profit.

Here's another technique fast food restaurants frequently use. It's called "bundling," or "packaging."

It's where they combine a sandwich, a drink, and fries, then throw in a couple of "bonus" items, like maybe a cookie and a toy. They put it all together in one package, and give it a name like "Value Meal."

They'll charge you less for that package than what each of those items purchased separately would have cost, but the total dollar amount you spend will be higher.

And, since there were no marketing costs involved, other than the cost of the items, themselves, it's pure profit, and it goes straight to their bottom line.

Just ask yourself this question: "What additional products or services do you have that would be natural complements to what your customers initially buy from you?"

Well, you know the answer to that and I won't go into all the details here.

Do these things seem like common sense to you? Well, they probably do. But as I mentioned before, it's surprising how few businesses make effective use of these three simple principles.

Think about it. In reality, you have an obligation to your customers... the people who trust you to provide them good quality products and services, give them sound advice and who hand over their hard-earned money to you... to make sure they get the very best value, the best use and the most enjoyment from their original purchase.

And if you have additional items, either products or services, that can enhance their value, their use or their enjoyment, then your obligation is to do everything that's reasonable and ethical to see that they at least have the option of taking advantage of those items.

Again, it's playing the numbers game. Some will take advantage of your offer, and some won't. But at least you will have given them the opportunity, and you will have fulfilled your obligation to them.

You haven't made the decision for them. You've given them a choice, and you've let them decide.

If you come across as sincere, they'll not see you as being pushy, but they'll realize that you are really trying to do them a favor... to help them get more value, more use, and more benefit from their decision and their purchase.

And they'll come back to do business with you again, and again, and will refer others to you, as well.

Up-selling, cross-selling and bundling... these are only three of more than a dozen immediate, profit-producing methods you can use to skyrocket your business to the next level.

If you do nothing more than find a way to incorporate these three techniques in your business (which you should be able to do within the next twenty-four hours), you'll blast your profits completely through the roof.

Think about it... increasing your sales... increasing your *profits*... without increasing your expenses. It's an exciting concept, and it can add an *immediate* twenty, thirty, even forty percent or more, *in pure profits* to your bottom line!

Now, let's move on to the third way to grow your restaurant business...

Get Your Customers To Buy From You More Often

In other words, increase the frequency of their purchases. Get them to come back, give them reasons to *want* to come back and to continue doing business with you. The longer your customers go between purchases from you, the more chance they have of buying from your competition.

It's like, "Out of sight, out of mind." You need to constantly stay in front of your customers with information, and notices of changes or updates regarding the products or services they've purchased from you that can affect them. And you need to tell them about new products, new lines, special incentives and other offers that might benefit them.

The idea is to make it so attractive to do business with you, that they wouldn't even consider going anywhere else.

What you really want to do, is lead your customers to the inescapable and undeniable conclusion, that they would have to be completely out of their minds to even consider doing business with anyone else but you, regardless of the selection of products or menus you provide, the prices you charge, your location, or the relationship they may have with the business they're currently doing business with. Sure, a customer isn't always going to want to eat your style of food in your location, but you want them to think twice before they go somewhere else.

Let me give you an extreme example. When I was a kid, my mom gave me this gadget called a Road Whiz. This was way before GPS became a "thing". What the Road Whiz did was have all the major US roadways programmed in with food and gas locations. You would enter what state you were in, what highway and direction you were travelling and exit mile marker or exit number you were at or just past.

Then, Road Whiz allowed you to program in various food types and what the distance was to the next one on the highway you were on. Very much like a GPS or travel app we have today.

I fell in love with a large chain of Country Stores which offered that gluttonous southern fare I loved, especially Chicken Fried Steak for dinner and Biscuits and Gravy for breakfast. They have both. Well, on a trip driving from home in Rhode Island down I-95 South towards Orlando, Florida, mom and I stopped for EVERY meal at one of these havens of deliciousness.

This level of repeat business is what we are trying to create for your restaurant.

Let me give you more real-life examples of how this works: One of the clients I consult with owns a restaurant. And for his business customers who like to take their clients to lunch, he offers a certain

72

number of lunches for a pre-paid, discounted price.

By doing this, he "locks in" his customer, gets his money up-front and makes it convenient for everyone. The customer simply signs the check, which includes the tip. No money changes hands during or after the lunch, and new customers are constantly being introduced to his restaurant. As a result, many of those new customers take advantage of the same arrangement for their clients.

Here's another example. The car wash where I take my cars offers a special pre-paid, discounted card, that's good for a certain number of car washes. It's a great deal for me because I save money, and I can take my car to be washed, even if the last couple of dollars I had gone the way of the Dodo bird.

And when my card is filled, I've got a free wax job coming. It's a good deal for the car wash too, because they've gotten their money up front, and have locked me out of the competition.

Here's one more. The store my assistant buys shoes from offers a "points" program. Every so often, she receives a notice in the mail informing her of how many points she's accumulated. Now, she may not have been to that store for quite a while, but when she gets that notice and sees the credit she has coming, she nearly always makes it back to that store within just a couple of days. And she hardly ever leaves empty-handed.

Airlines offer upgrades and mileage bonuses for those who fly with them on a regular basis. And countless other businesses offer similar programs as well.

Now, let us apply this concept to your restaurant business. What can you think of that you could do, that will endear your customers to you? To lock them in, and get them coming back more often, and even refer others to do business with you?

Do you have an educational newsletter or special informative reports that you periodically send them that keeps them updated?

Do you send postcards, or do you have a website that keeps them informed of new items and promotions?

Do you hold special "Customer Appreciation Sales" or events? How about a frequent buyer club for your more loyal customers? What about a Referral Reward system that recognizes or

compensates your customers for referring their friends?

You've got to let your customers know that you value them, that you appreciate them, that you want them to come back, and you want to make doing business with you fun, risk-free, rewarding, and easy.

Well, I'm sure you can see that the ideas are unlimited.

In our coaching programs, we go into great detail and discuss more than two-dozen very specific strategies that create an almost magnetic effect, that keeps your customers returning time and time again.

We lead you by the hand and help you develop personalized and effective strategies that keep them saying, "I'll be back"... strategies that keep them "insulated" from, and locked out of your competition.

Now let's talk about the fourth method you can use to grow your business. And that is, to...

Extend Your Customers' "Average Buying Lifetime"

We call that, "Customer Retention."

Here's what I mean: How long, on average, do the people who buy from you, your customers, remain your customers?

In other words, how long do they continue doing business with you before they move on? Are they one-time buyers? Do they stay with you for a year, five years or ten years? Have you ever stopped to figure it out? This is an important step and one that we'll be discussing in more detail in later pages.

Next, what are you doing in your restaurant business *right now*, to make sure your customers *continue* doing business with you? If you don't have a strategic plan, a *working system* in place, you are going to lose a certain percent of your current customers to the competition.

There's no question about it. Your competition... *right now*... *right this very minute* is making plans and taking steps to take your customers away from you.

The question for you, is not, "What are you going to do about it?" The *real* question is, "What are you *currently* doing about it?" "What are you doing about it *right now?*"

What plans... what *systems* do you have in place to keep your customers from defecting to the competition?

Let's talk about your customers for a minute. Are they *thrilled* enough with the products you offer and the services they receive from you to continue doing business with you year after year?

What if you answered "yes" to that question?
My next questions would be, "Are you sure?" "How do you know?"

"Where did you get your

information?" "How reliable is it?"

"Can you explain in detail, the *system* you have in place for finding out?"

Notice that I said, "Are they *thrilled* enough?" Not "are they *satisfied* enough?" You see, there's a big difference between being *thrilled* and being *satisfied*.

Last year, more than 200 million Americans stopped doing business with companies that they were "satisfied" with. And sixty percent of so-called "satisfied" customers switch companies or brands on a regular basis.

As a restaurant owner, you have to thrill your customers and help them build trust in your business. Unfortunately, most business owners simply don't understand it. Let's take a look at what the potential cost could be to you if you fail to do these things:

Let's say that you make $200 in sales per year from your average customer. This may be modest depending on your restaurant, but let's use it to illustrate this example.

And let's say that for any number of reasons, 100 customers stop doing business with you each year. They may die or move away. They may no longer have need for your products or services, they may switch companies, have a relative in the business, or possibly have a bad experience with someone in your company.

Or, they may just simply disagree with some policy or procedure you might have. It could be a falling out with a staff member or employee, a personality conflict, miscommunication, a problem they had with one of your products, or perhaps a feeling of neglect from you or someone in your business. It really doesn't matter what the reason, they just stop doing business with you.

Well, those 100 customers no longer paying you $200 this year just cost you $20,000. But, that's not all. What if those 100 customers tell 5 others about their experience with you?

That's an additional 500 potential customers who won't be doing business with you this year (or maybe ever, for that matter).

And if each of them spent an average of $200, that's $100,000 you won't be receiving from them, *PLUS* the $20,000 you lost on your existing customers who left.

That brings the total in lost income to *$120,000 in just one year!* It's not unusual for some businesses to bring in a hundred (or

more) new customers each month. That's twelve hundred-plus, customers a year. And they end up only netting a 150 or 200 increase at year-end (sometimes not even that).

Well, what happened to the other more than 1,000 customers? Where did they go? Surely, they all didn't die or move away.

But, you know, most restaurant owners don't concern themselves with what, or whom they've lost. They just focus on their net gain. They figure that if they finish the year with more customers or more sales than they started with, they're ahead.

Now, let's suppose that you gave those 100 lost customers reasons… good, compelling, life or business enhancing reasons, to continue doing business with you this year.

And let's suppose each of them told those same five people about their now-positive experience with you.

Well, there's $20,000 you wouldn't have lost in the first place and another $100,000 you may possibly pick up from their referrals or by their word of mouth.

The point is, customers are important – *all* customers. In fact, they're critical. There's no question about it. You and I both know that. A business couldn't remain in business unless it has someone to buy its products and services.

Those "someone's" are people. Real people. People like you and like me. If you sell your products to the business community, remember, businesses don't buy from businesses.

People in business buy from other people in business. It's people that you market to. Not businesses.

Here's an interesting point: Most business owners know exactly how much they have tied up in furniture, fixtures, and equipment also known as FF&E. They can tell you, nearly to the penny, how much each item costs, how old it is, how much it's depreciated and what the remaining life expectancy is.

That's important information for any restaurant business to have. There's no question about it. But what's amazing is that very few business owners have any idea of what the value of their most important asset is… their customers.

Think about how this whole concept relates to your business, for a minute. What is it that you can do, *specifically*, to extend your customer's buying lifetime with you? Why not take a few minutes and answer these questions?

First of all, who are your customers … those who are buying from you now?

Who are their family members?

Do you know the names and ages of their spouse or children?

Do you know where they work?

What about their spouse or children?

What are their hobbies or interests?

Do you know why they purchased a certain type of product or service?

Do you know who their friends, neighbors or relatives are?

What about your staff or employees? Do you know how they treat or feel about your customers?

Do they, or do you, for that matter, have *favorite* customers? What makes them a "favorite?" Is it how much they spend? How often they come in? Their personality? And how do you treat those customers? Any different than the others?

Do you have regular staff meetings and talk about how to think like a customer?

What would you want if you were a prospect considering making purchases from you for the first time? Or maybe an existing customer considering giving repeat business to your establishment or organization?

Or, perhaps considering referring a friend, a family member or an acquaintance?

Do you have a training system in place to teach your staff how to handle or deal with difficult customers? Short-tempered customers? Analytical customers?

Do you have a plan for moving people up the "Loyalty Ladder?" From Suspect to Prospect to Diner. Then on to Advocate. And, finally to convert them into Raving Fans?

When a customer stops doing business with you, do you know why? Do you have a *system* in place to find out?

What would you have to do differently to get your customers to buy from you for, say, 5 ½ years, instead of just 5 years?

Believe me, if you will actually take the time to go through these questions and formulate answers for them, and then incorporate that information into your business practices, you can work wonders towards extending the buying lifetime of your customers.

And as a result, you'll add *significant* profits to your bottom line. We've covered a lot of ground and a lot of ideas, so far. So, let's

pause for a minute, and recap what we've discussed up to this point. There are four primary ways to grow a Restaurant business.

First, **get more customers**. And as I mentioned, this is a vital step. But it's also the most difficult and the most costly.

Second, **get your customers to spend more money with you**... increase the average check value of each sale. And remember that this is the fastest and the easiest way to add immediate profits to your bottom line.

Third, **get your customers coming back to buy from you more often**.

And, fourth, **extend your customers' buying lifetime**. Find ways to retain them, keep them as customers and keep them coming back as long as you possibly can. It's really pretty simple. Nearly everything you do to build and grow your restaurant can be slotted under one of these four categories. As I mentioned earlier, there are more than two-dozen ways to apply these concepts and build your business, but for now, if you'll work on these four primary methods, you'll absolutely run circles around your competitors.

As you take a good, close-up look at these four areas, you'll see that what it really boils down to, is effectively marketing your business to your customers and potential customers.

In other words, the success of your business enterprise depends, largely, on how effective your marketing system is.

And that means that if you want your business to excel... to really excel... if you want to virtually eliminate your competition, and become the dominating force in your marketplace, then you've got to begin thinking of yourself as being in the *marketing* business, not in the product or service selling business.

In effect, you need to consider yourself as the head of a marketing organization that sells the products and services that your business offers.

Once you begin operating effectively at that point, you'll find that your job becomes much easier and much more enjoyable, and your prospects and customers will begin seeking you out and referring others to you, rather than you chasing after them. The net result will be that your marketing costs will plummet, and your profits will skyrocket!

"Only a life lived for others is a life worthwhile."

Albert Einstein

7

HOW MUCH ARE YOUR CUSTOMERS REALLY WORTH?

Determining The Lifetime Profit
Value Of Your Customers

There's not much debate about this fact: Your existing customers are your most valuable assets. The question is, how much are they worth?

How much money... how much *profit* will you realize from each of your customers, over their "buying lifetime" with you?

This is such an important concept, and I can't say it strongly enough, that just knowing and understanding this one thing can have a bigger impact on your business than just about anything else you can do.

Once you understand it, a whole new set of factors will come into play and can absolutely revolutionize the way you look at your business, the way you *do* business, and the profits you'll generate as a result. Let me give you an example to explain what I mean.

Let's say that your average sale is $50. And let's say that your average customer buys from you 4 times per year.

So, from those four transactions, you realize $200 in income. And let's say that this customer does business with you on average, for 10 years. Over that 10-year period (or their "lifetime" of doing business with you), that average customer has been worth $2,000 in income to you.

Now, let's expand this example to a theoretical base of 1,000 customers and see what it means. Those 1,000 customers at $200 a year net you an annual income of $200,000.

Let's assume that with the proper programs in place, that you're able to increase each of the 4 ways to grow your restaurant that we discussed earlier, by only 10 percent. Here's what happens:

First, the number of customers you have increases from 1,000 to 1,100.

Next, the average transaction amount per sale increases from $50 to $55.

Third, the average number of purchases per customer increases from 4 times 4.4 times.

So, the annual income from your customer base will increase from $200,000 ($50 x 4 transactions x 1,000 customers) to $266,200 ($55 x 4.4 x 1,100 customers). That's an increase of $66,200 a year!

That's a huge increase!

But if you think that's exciting, wait till you see what happens if you were to extend your customer's buying lifetime by just 10 percent.

Let's say that your customers stay with you for 10 years, on average. Your lifetime value from those customers over that period of time would normally be $2,000,000. But, if you can extend that 10 years by just 10 percent to 11 years, your total dollar value from these customers will increase from $2,000,000 to $2,928,200 ($266,200 x 11 years)!

An increase of $928,200... nearly a million dollars! That's a *major* increase!

But that's not all. Let's say that you put an effective referral generating system in place and that just 10 percent of your 1,000 customers send you a referral with a buying profile the same as your average customer.

That's an additional 100 customers who will bring you an income of another $266,200 over the 11 years ($55 x 4.4 renewals x 100 customers x 11 years).

Total it all up, and you just made an additional $1,194,400! That's an average of $1,085,818 per year over the 11 years! Sound impossible? Well, it's not. And it's not all that difficult, either. It can be done by simply increasing each of the four areas by only 10 percent!

Now, how hard would that be to do in your business? Could you realistically, and with some help, increase each of the four areas we discussed, by ten percent? What about twenty percent?

Some of the restaurant businesses we consult with, after realizing the power of this key concept, and the others that we've discussed, have increased their businesses by as much as a hundred percent, or more in less than a year.

Maybe the numbers and figures I've discussed are realistic for you and your restaurant, and maybe they're not. And maybe you can't increase each of the areas by the same percentage. That's okay. That doesn't matter.

The point is you probably have room for improvement in one, or more of the four areas. And if you want your restaurant to be a viable force in the marketplace, and to give you the lifestyle, the satisfaction and the income you want, you're going to have to take some proactive steps.

Knowing The Value Of Your Customers Influences The Way You Treat Them

As I mentioned before, just knowing how much your customers are worth to you can be invaluable and can help you in several ways.

First of all, we know that people don't do business with the same restaurant forever. They stop doing business or change where they eat for a variety of reasons, and we've already discussed some of those.

But, if you just know, for instance, that your typical customer stays with you for say, ten years, on average, that they're not just a one or two-time sale, you may begin to treat them differently.

You may treat them with more respect, more kindness, more courtesy. You may give them some form of special treatment. And you may even invite them to special, invitation-only, preferred customer seminars or events.

In other words, once you begin to see your customers in a different light, you may begin to do things differently in order to get them to stay longer as customers.

Next, if you know what the Lifetime Profit Value of your customers is, you'll probably discover that you can spend far more to acquire a new customer than you originally thought.

In other words, if your average customer is worth $2,000 in income to you, you can, theoretically, afford to spend up to $2,000 to bring in a new customer and still break even.

In theory, you could spend that $2,000 and still make a profit on the other "back-end" products that you might be able to sell them.

And, if you put an effective referral-generating program in place, you can spend that same $2,000, and make your profits on the referrals they generate.

You and I both know that it's unrealistic to think that you can really afford to spend the full amount of your lifetime income (in this case, $2,000), to get each new customer. And I'm certainly not suggesting that.

In reality, you *can't* spend the entire $2,000. You've got to be concerned about things like overhead, cash-flow and reserves. You can't spend money you don't have.

And, you have to make sure that the customers you attract, at least match the profile of your average customers, or perhaps are even a little better than average.

There are a number of other things that you need to be aware of, as well, such as, "Cost of Acquisition," "Cost of Retention," understanding your margins, and calculating the Marginal Net Worth of your customers.

Unfortunately, we don't have time to cover them in sufficient detail, here.

Knowing The Value Of Your Customers Influences How Much You Can Spend To Get A New One, Or Keep An Existing One

What it really comes down to are two questions: How much

can you *afford* to spend, and how much are you *willing* to spend to attract new business?

You may find that you can and are willing to spend five or six times what your competitors spend. And if they're not willing to keep up with you, your business may just explode and leave them in the dust.

Just knowing what your *margins* are, and that you could, if you had to, spend up to that $2,000 amount and still break even, gives you a *tremendous* edge over your competition.

Here's another real-life example: My family and I have a favorite restaurant we like to go to about twice a month. And our meals typically come to about $30. So $30 times 24 meals adds up to $720 in gross sales for the year.

Let's suppose that we continue to patronize that restaurant for, say, 10 years. That's our buying lifetime with that particular restaurant. That gives the restaurant a total of $7,200 in sales.

If over that 10-year period, we refer 10 people, 5 of whom become regular customers (and that's not very many in 10 years), who have spending patterns similar to ours, they'll spend an additional $36,000. (That's 5 people, times $7,200 a year.)

Add that to the $7,200 that we spent, and we've been responsible for generating $43,200 for that restaurant. Even after deducting expenses for overhead, salaries and food costs, the restaurant still realizes a pretty substantial number of profit dollars from the efforts of just one couple.

Restaurant Example	
A. Amount of average sale	$ 30

B. No. of sales/year/customer (2 x per month)	24
C. Gross income per year per customer (A x B)	$ 720
D. No. of years customer patronizes restaurant	10
E. Gross income over buying lifetime (C x D)	$ 7,200
F. No. of referrals from customer over buying lifetime	10
G. % of referrals who become a customer	50 %
H. Referrals who become customers (G x F)	5
I. Gross income from referrals (E x H)	$ 36,000
J. Total value of a loyal customer (E + I)	**$ 43,200**

Now, here's a question: Could that restaurant afford to give away a free meal to attract a new customer? Keep in mind that two of us are spending $30, so one meal costs $15, and out of that, about a third of it (or, maybe $5) is profit.

So, the meal really only costs the restaurant $10 for the two meals, and only part of that $10 goes to cover the cost of the food.
The rest of the expense is in overhead, which would have to be paid whether or not a meal was served.

Well, of course the answer is yes, they *can* afford to give away a free meal. Not only that, but they can afford to do a number of other things to not only attract new customers, but more important, make their existing customers feel more appreciated and more special. And you know, when someone feels noticed and important, appreciated and special, it's just natural that they'll want to return.

Let's imagine, for a minute, that you are a long-time, faithful customer of a certain restaurant. And you brought your family, your clients or your business associates with you to eat there on a regular basis.

How would *you* feel, if sometime, the manager of the restaurant were to offer you and your party a free dessert as a special appreciation gift for your loyalty and for the extra business you brought them? Do you think that little display of appreciation would cause you to want to return again? I think it's pretty safe to say that it probably would.

And what about the people who were with you? How do you think they would feel? Do you think they would want to go back to that restaurant? Sure they would. What do you think the restaurant's hard costs of those desserts would be? Do you think the restaurant would lose any money on that gesture?

Well, it's not likely. You see, once you know how much profit your customers are worth to you, long term, then, and only then, can you determine how much you can afford to give away, or to spend, to get new customers, or to keep your existing customers coming back. And you can begin to experiment with different offers to see which ones work best.

Now, here's another thought. Let's say that the owner of that restaurant runs an ad or does a mailing to attract new customers.

And let's say he spends $1,000 for the ad or the mailing, and two couples come in for dinner, and each spends $30.

Well, he's taken in a total of $60. But the ad costs were $1,000. So, what does he do? What would his competition do?

Does he consider the ad or mail campaign a loser... a total bust... and stop running it? That's what most business people do.

But what about you? What would you do? Well, if you understand the concept of Lifetime Profit Value and Marginal Net Worth, you'll probably think differently.

When you consider the Lifetime Value of those customers and realize that with the proper care and attention those customers could be responsible for $43,200 each, or $86,400 for the two of them, it changes the picture.

Of course, those numbers are gross revenue figures, and you have to deduct for expenses. And it's over a 10-year period. But, still, that represents a significant amount of money. And all from a $1,000 ad. An ad that most business owners would have given up on.

Now, I'm not saying that you have to settle for and be happy with low response rates for your ads. Certainly, you don't. You should always try to improve your ads, your letters, your offers... and give good, compelling reasons and benefits for someone to do business with you.

That's an entire subject, itself, and one we don't have time to discuss in great detail here. But one we take very seriously and spend considerable time on in our workshops and coaching programs.

Let's go back and think about our restaurant example for a minute. Did this idea of not stopping an ad just because it didn't break even, or produce a profit for you sound unusual? Different? Strange? Well, maybe to some people, in some businesses.

But, supermarkets and department stores use their own adaptation of this technique all the time. You've probably heard it referred to as a "loss leader."

What they do is advertise a few products at, or below cost to bring new customers into their store, knowing that the customer will usually buy more products once they're in the store.

And also knowing, that unless they get someone to visit their store in the first place, they could never stand a chance of making additional or repeat sales or getting referrals from them. And additional and repeat sales to existing customers are generally easier to make, and usually always bring higher profit margins.

Just remember this important point:

The first sale means nothing... unless you're planning on going out of business next week. You've got to consider the Lifetime Profit Value...what your customer is worth to you, if you really want to be successful.

Now, what about your restaurant? How can you apply this concept of Lifetime Profit Value?

Well, the first thing you can do is determine what the amount of your average income per sale is. The Lifetime Profit Value Calculator below is provided for you to use in calculating the Lifetime Profit Value of your own customers. Fill out with your current figures to get an idea of how much your customers are worth to you.

The LPV Of Your Customers (Actual)

A. Amount of average sale	$
B. No. of sales/year/customer (2 x per month)	$
C. Gross income per year per customer (A x B)	$
D. No. of years customer patronizes restaurant	%
E. Gross income over buying lifetime (C x D)	$
F. No. of referrals from customer over buying lifetime	$
G. % of referrals who become a customer	$

H. Referrals who become customers (G x F)	$
I. Gross income from referrals (E x H)	$
J. Total value of a loyal customer (E + I)	%

The calculator below is provided so you can calculate what kind of a difference it will make to your business if you increased each of the areas by 10 percent.

Keep in mind as you do these calculations, that this is a very simplified calculation. In our consulting sessions, we get very detailed and take into consideration many more areas. So the results you'll see in actuality will be dramatically increased. But for a simple and easy to demonstrate a way to determine your customers' value to you, these basic calculators will do quite nicely.

8

THE BIGGEST RESTAURANT GROWTH STRATEGY ONLY "THE BIG BOYS" USE

Like it or not, Social media is a major component of life nowadays. Some people spend more time on social media than they do talking with people in real life.

More and more people are staying up to date with the news through mobile devices like smart phones and tablets. We now have in our pockets computers that are more powerful than the original ones which launched astronauts into space.

Standard app category on most smartphones?? Social media like Facebook, Twitter, Yelp, Foursquare and others. Facebook is the proverbial elephant in the corner of the room. They have more than 2 billion active monthly users. That is billion with a B.

This certainly begs the question: can the average restaurant owner, and specifically, YOUR restaurant benefit from all of these users?

The answer is a very big YES! That is, if you know how to do it the most effective way...

Let's start with having a Facebook page. Does your restaurant have one? If not, here is how:

- Go to facebook.com/pages/create.
- Click to choose a Page type.
- Fill out the required information.
- Click Get Started and follow the on-screen instructions.

Once you have this setup, you need to share this will everyone who comes into your restaurant. Ask people to "Check In" on Facebook when they eat there.

This starts to build what we call Social Proof. The more Social Proof you can generate, the easier it will be for you to get more diners in the door. More on this a little later.

Many people will post pictures inside the restaurant and definitely pictures of the food. This becomes the easiest marketing and advertising you can ever create and for no out of pocket investment.

The $5.00 a Day Full Restaurant Recipe

If I were to tell you for around $150 or so per month you could advertise to your perfect customer and experience an increase in customers AND revenue, you might be a bit skeptical.

How?
Easy.

You simply go onto your Facebook page for your restaurant and create a simple post about your restaurant, a special event, a promo or any other piece of interest.

Once you do that, you can then go into your Facebook account and "Boost" the post. Boosting is the Facebook term to have your post shown to whatever specific audience you want.

Want to show a promo about a Free Appetizer just to the fans of your page? You can do that.

Want to offer a Buy One Get One Free entrée promo to fans of your style of restaurant who live within a 5-mile radius of your restaurant? You can do that too.

The possibilities can soon become endless. Facebook will let you advertise to people in your area who are similar to your customers. Facebook will seek out people who have similar interests and tastes as your existing customers or ones who like your Facebook page.

Imagine being able to tap into an audience of diners who have never heard of you but who a predisposed to your cuisine and live within miles of your restaurant. Could this help you fill your restaurant on a Tuesday lunch when your dining room is not at full capacity? You betcha!

How about advertising a Birthday promo to people celebrating a birthday this month? You can do that on Facebook too just like Cindy who owns an American style restaurant.

She spent $500 in advertising on Facebook and targeted birthday folks in very close proximity to her restaurant. The first month this campaign was in effect, 91 new customers were generated for her restaurant.

She kept doing this every month and by the third month, there were 150 new people coming in EVERY month to redeem their birthday promotion. This created an additional $1,500 a month every month.

The question is not would you spend $500 a month to generate $1,500 a month of additional revenue but rather **how many times** a month would you spend $500 to make $1,500?

The possibilities are endless and through smart and specific strategies, you can attract a highly receptive crowd of diners and profit from them immediately. Not to mention the Lifetime Value we discussed earlier in the book.

For more information about Cindy and how she generated these \ new leads or to see other restaurants successfully leveraging the power of Facebook, go to: http://bit.ly/fb-ems

"It is not the strongest of the species that survives, nor the most intelligent, but the one most responsive to change."

Charles Darwin

9

MARKETING TO YOUR RESTAURANT CUSTOMER BASE USING A SIMPLE VIP LOYALTY PROGRAM

I remember back when I started in the restaurant industry having a loyalty program where a customer would a punch on a punch card for $20 spent in the restaurant.

Once they accumulated the required number of punches, they could redeem it towards a meal. This was a VIP Loyalty Program in its most basic form.

Nowadays, there are as many different forms of VIP Loyalty Programs as there are restaurants using. Time and time again, having a customer base to market to will set you farther ahead than your competition.

Now you don't have to spend tens of thousands of dollars setting one up or maintaining one or maintaining the logistics like many of the chain restaurants do.

I have found there is a very easy and highly effective way to utilize a VIP Loyalty Rewards Program. That is through a text program.

Here's how it works: You advertise your VIP Program in your restaurant and tell your customers to text a code to a specific number. When they do, they will be rewarded with a gift.

What kind of gift? It could be anything you want: a free appetizer, a buy one get one free, free dessert, 25% off the entire check or my personal favorite, a Free Birthday Entrée.

You remember in the last chapter we talked about using Facebook to advertise your restaurant. Imagine using Facebook to advertise your VIP Rewards Club.

I know right now you are saying, John, why would we want to do that if we are adverting the Free Entrée on Facebook? Well, on Facebook, you own nothing. Meaning, that customer is Facebook's customer, not yours.

Sure, they may come to your restaurant and become your customer, but at the end of the day, they are Facebook's.

But, when you get them to join your VIP Rewards Program via text, you now own them as they are a part of your list. Yes, they are still a Facebook customer, but now they are truly your customer as well.

Imagine this, it is the slow season in your restaurant and it is the slowest period of the week. Maybe it's a Monday lunch or a Sunday dinner, but whatever period it is, you still have the electric running, staff to pay and food sitting in your walk-ins while there is no one in your dining room.

Well, with your VIP Rewards Program in place, you now have a list of people who already like your restaurant and you can send them a text message to come in at that time.

When you have several hundred to multiple thousands of people in your program, which is very easy to obtain, even the smallest of response will bring people into your restaurant.

Look, people are attached to their cell phone so much that medical science has declared something they call Phantom Vibration Syndrome a real thing. Look it up on Wikipedia. They state:

"Phantom vibration syndrome or phantom ringing syndrome is the perception that one's mobile phone is vibrating or ringing when it is not ringing. Other terms for this concept include ringxiety (a portmanteau of ring and anxiety), fauxcellarm (a portmanteau of "faux" /fō/ meaning "fake" or "false" and "cellphone" and "alarm" pronounced similarly to "false alarm") and phonetom (a portmanteau of phone and phantom). According to Dr. Michael Rothberg, the term is not a syndrome, but is better characterised as a tactile hallucination since the brain perceives a sensation that is not actually present."

With so many people engaged with their cell phones, it makes sense to utilize a strategy like the VIP Loyalty Rewards Club because your audience will most certainly get the message.

In fact, a report by Retail Dive, a company which covers retail industry news and provide original analysis, says that texting, also known as SMS, is 8X more effective than email.

8 TIMES MORE EFFECTIVE!!

Wow! Now, I am a huge proponent of building an email database of your customers but I am also a huge fan of strategies which produce tremendous results including SMS.

Think about it, how many times have you put off checking or doing something in your email but you get a text and you check it out. I do it too. Email is often not nearly as novel as it used to be back in the "You've Got Mail" days and quite frankly, has become a huge distraction and often a necessary evil.

I don't know about you but I don't want to be in the necessary evil category but that is a discussion for a different time.

Setting up a VIP Loyalty Club will result in more customer visits guaranteed.

To see how your restaurant will benefit from a VIP Rewards Loyalty Club, go to:
http://bit.ly/ems-sms

"When inspiration does not come to me, I go halfway to meet it."

Sigmund Freud

EPILOGUE

Where Do You Go From Here

Congratulations for making it this far. You have now been exposed to some of the most powerful and effective techniques, concepts and ideas available for succeeding in restaurant business.

But no matter how good these ideas are, just being exposed to them is not enough. You must also do something with them. In order for you to get the most value out of this material, you might want to consider developing a step-by-step action plan. An effective and results producing plan should consist of 5 areas:

1. EVALUATION

Ideas are nothing more than ideas until they are put into action. Once acted on, they have the potential to literally turn around a struggling business or help an already successful restaurant become even more dynamic and successful.

But before a person runs out and implements a new-found idea, they should first take the time to evaluate their operation to determine just what areas are most lacking and could use the most attention.

You have the potential of making the most improvement in your own restaurant if you will take the time to identify and work on the area of greatest need, first.

101

2. RESEARCH

Once you've identified your greatest needs and placed them in priority order, you can begin to search out available solutions. Be on an opportunity lookout. The material in this manual is just the beginning of the many places you can find good, usable, and practical ideas.

Don't turn any ideas away just because you think they might not pertain to your restaurant or the way you operate. Capture them and then apply step number three.

3. PERSONALIZATION

As you encounter new ideas, keep an open mind. Study them. Analyze them. And think them through. Ask yourself if an application can be made to your specific situation by simply changing or modifying part of the concept or idea.

If a certain illustration uses a certain type of product or service for the example, but you don't sell that product or service, a simple adjustment might be all that's needed.

The material in the book is designed to illustrate concepts, and only uses certain types of products as examples to make various points.

4. IMPLEMENTATION

Just as a membership in a health club won't do its owner any good unless he or she goes to the club and participates in the exercise program, so too, with the information in this book.

It's of no practical use unless it is implemented. It's easy to come up with good ideas and develop plans, but where most people get bogged down is when it comes to putting them into action. It's not always easy, but if you're going to truly be successful, you must do whatever it takes to act on your plans.

5. REVIEW

After you've worked with your new ideas for a period of time, stop and evaluate how things are working. You may need to make some adjustments so you can continue to see improvement.

Sometimes, an idea you thought was great doesn't work out at all. That's okay, don't continue using it. Just scrap it and move on to something else.

On the other hand, if you find an idea that works well, see if you can refine it, or "plus" it to make it even more effective.

That's all there is to it. Sounds simple enough to say, but in reality, there's a lot to do. The plain and truthful facts are, that most people simply won't take the time and effort to do the things we've just discussed. That's unfortunate on one hand because they could be even more successful than they are now.

On the other hand, their failure to take action is good for you. Because if it's you that does these things and not them, it will be you who realizes the success.

Now you have the tools…

GO FOR IT!